Graded 5 - up

LIFE IN THE TIME OF
HARALD HARDRADA
and the Vikings

Peter Speed

Illustrations by Richard Hook

RSVP
**RAINTREE
STECK-VAUGHN**
P U B L I S H E R S
The Steck-Vaughn Company

Austin, Texas

Published by Raintree Steck-Vaughn Publishers, an imprint of Steck-Vaughn Company.

A Mirabel Book
Produced by Cynthia Parzych Publishing, Inc.
648 Broadway, N.Y., N.Y. l0012
Edited by: John Gilbert

Printed and bound in Belgium by Proost International Book Production

1 2 3 4 5 6 7 8 9 0 Pl 98 97 96 95 94 93

Library of Congress Cataloging-in-Publication Data

Speed, Peter
    Life in the time of Harald Hardrada and the Vikings / written by Peter Speed; illustrated by Richard Hook.
        p. cm. — (Life in the time of)
"A Mirabel book"—T.p. verso.
Includes index.
    Summary: Describes the origins, activities, and invasions of the Vikings.
    ISBN 0-8114-3353-6
    1. Vikings — Social life and customs—Juvenile literature. 2. Northmen—Social life and customs—Juvenile literature. 3. Harald III Harsrasi, King of Norway, 1015-1066—Juvenile literature {1. Vikings.}
I. Hook, Richard, ill. II. Title. III.Title: Harald Hardrada and the Vikings. IV. Series.
DL31.S64 1993
940'.04395—dc20
92-5818
CIP
    AC

NOTE TO THE READER:

For the sake of authenticity, we have used the Norwegian spelling of the name "Harald," instead of the American adaptation "Harold."

COVER ILLUSTRATIONS:

Front: A Viking warrior and two working women, in the background is a ship with a raiding party.

Back: The god Thor fighting the World Serpent and at left, a merchant on horseback, a women herding goats against a background of Viking ships under sail.

PHOTO CREDITS:

Bridgeman Art Library: 9
British Museum: 8, 20 top, 21, 25 top, 25 bottom, 36, 47, 49
Cassady, Richard: 11, 27 top, 29 top, 43, 51 top, 58 [courtesy of the city of Bayeux, France], 59 [courtesy of the city of Bayeux, France]
Chang, Heidi: 17
D.O.E. / Canadian Parks Service: 44
Sonia Halliday Photographs: 51
University Museum of National Antiquities, Oslo: 27 bottom
Werner Forman Archive: 14

Contents

CHAPTER 1

Brother to St. Olaf

There was once a king of Norway known as Olaf the Stout. He had three brothers, much younger than himself, named Guthrum, Halfdan, and Harald.

One day, when Olaf was playing with his little brothers, he set each of them on his knee in turn and made faces at them. Guthrum and Halfdan cried out in fear, but Harald, the youngest, who was only three, reached out his hand and tweaked Olaf's whiskers. Olaf laughed and told the child he would be very vengeful one day, which proved right. Harald grew up with an unforgiving nature, so much so that he earned himself the nickname "Hardrada," which means "hard ruler" or "ruthless."

Another time, when the family was standing beside a lake, Olaf asked the three boys what they would like most in the world. Pointing to a large piece of land with ten farms on it, Guthrum said he would like all the grain from it every year. Halfdan said he would like so many cattle that when they came to drink, they would stand shoulder to shoulder all around the lake. For his part, Harald said he would like so many soldiers that they would eat all Halfdan's cattle in one meal. Olaf turned to his mother and told her she was bringing up a king. Again Olaf's prediction was right, for many years later, Harald became king of Norway.

Olaf was disliked by his Norwegian subjects. Many of them were pagans, and Olaf tried to make them become Christians, killing or torturing those who refused. In the end, Canute, king of Denmark, attacked Olaf, whereupon the Norwegians helped Canute. Olaf fled to Sweden, gathered an army, and in the year A.D. 1030 led it into Norway, hoping to regain his kingdom. Harald, who by then was fifteen, badly wanted to join his brother's army, but Olaf said he was not strong enough to hold a sword. Harald answered that he would tie it to his wrist, and Olaf gave way.

Olaf did not command many soldiers, so when he fought the rebels at Sticklestad, near Trondheim, he was defeated and killed. His people buried him, but dug him up some months later to give him a more honorable resting place. They were amazed to see that the body had not decayed, while his hair and nails had continued to grow, just as if Olaf were still alive. Furthermore, sick people who came to the tomb were cured. Because of these miracles, Olaf was made a saint.

Harald escaped from the Battle of Sticklestad, badly wounded. A peasant cared for him until he recovered, after which he had many amazing adventures in Russia and Byzantium. Eventually, he returned to Norway, where he became

king, and it was from here that he set out to attempt the conquest of England.

The young Harald pulls King Olaf's whiskers.

CHAPTER 2

Who Were the Vikings?

Memorial stone to a Viking hero. Below is his ship. At the top, his soul rides to Valhalla, the Viking heaven.

Olaf and his family were Vikings, otherwise known as Norsemen or Northmen. They were the people who lived in the Scandinavian countries of Norway, Sweden, Denmark, and their colonies from about A.D. 800 to around 1100. The word "Viking" means "pirate" or "raider." Not all Vikings, of course, were fierce, cruel adventurers, but many of them were.

It is sometimes difficult to find out what the Vikings were like and what they did. The problem is that they wrote very little, so they have left us no books, letters, or diaries. We have to use other sources.

Archaeologists have excavated many Viking sites and have found a great deal, for when a Viking died, some of his goods, such as weapons, armor, tools, and jewelry, were buried with him. The most exciting graves that have been unearthed contained two ships, called the Gokstad and the Oseberg ships, after the places where the ships were discovered. Houses have also been excavated and even a few entire towns, including Jorvik, better known today as York, in northern England.

Many hoards of silver have come to light, too. In times of danger, a Viking would bury his treasure, but if he was killed, his secret died with him, and his silver remained in the ground. Much of the silver consisted of coins, and the marks on them show when they were made and which country they came from. For example, there are hoards containing a great many English coins of about A.D. 1000, which shows that the English must have been giving the Vikings a lot of money at that time.

STONES AND SAGAS

To honor their dead, the people of Sweden and the island of Gotland used to erect memorial stones, with inscriptions. One stone put up by a man's widow, says, "He visited Jerusalem and died in Greece." Another, set up by four men in memory of their brother, Hrafn, says, "We had this stone painted and put up. We have also raised stones to Hrafn south of Rufstein. We went far into Aifur." Aifur was a cataract on the Dnieper River in southern Russia. Yet another stone, at Orkestad in Sweden, is to a man named Ulf. It says, "Ulf received danegeld three times in England. The first was paid by Tosti. Then Thorkel paid. Then Canute paid." Danegeld was a form of protection money, so we now know why the English were making such large payments to the Vikings.

Although the Vikings did not write much, monks in other countries kept chronicles. When the Vikings attacked, the monks reported exactly what happened. One of the most important of these historical records is the *Anglo-Saxon Chronicle*, written in England. The problem

A model of the Gokstad ship, named after the place in Norway where it was excavated over 100 years ago.

with the chronicles, however, is that the monks only met or heard about those Vikings who went raiding, and knew nothing of those who stayed peacefully at home.

One thing the *Anglo-Saxon Chronicle* tells us is that King Ethelred of England paid the Vikings large sums of danegeld, hoping to persuade them to leave his country in peace. You can see that we know about this protection money from three sources: the hoards of coins in Scandinavia, the Orkstad memorial stone, and the stories in the *Anglo-Saxon Chronicle*.

Many places in the British Isles have Viking names that end, for example, in "thorpe," which means "farm," and in "by," which means "village." Mablethorpe is "Malbert's farm"; Whitby is "Hviti's village"; Sowerby is "the village on muddy ground." Other Viking words are "beck," a stream, "force," a waterfall, "slack," a valley, and "thwaite," a clearing in a forest. The *Anglo-Saxon Chronicle* mentions that many Vikings settled in Britain without saying exactly where, but this can be discovered by marking all the places with Viking names on a map.

An interesting way of learning about the Vikings is to read the sagas, which are stories of heroic Viking leaders. We cannot, though, believe everything in the sagas since they make their heroes braver and their adventures more exciting than they really were. Another difficulty is that the sagas were not put into writing until the thirteenth century, hundreds of years after the many events they describe.

Until the sagas were written down, these tales were only kept alive by parents telling them to their sons and daughters. But it is unlikely that they changed much from generation to generation, for children object to favorite stories being altered. No modern parent would dare, for instance, to vary the tale of Goldilocks by saying, "Who's been sitting in my porridge?"

One man who wrote down the sagas was an Icelander named Snorri Sturluson (1179-1241), the author of several books on Viking kings, heroes, and gods. One of these books was a life of St. Olaf.

Silver penny from England.

9

CHAPTER 3

The Viking Lands and People

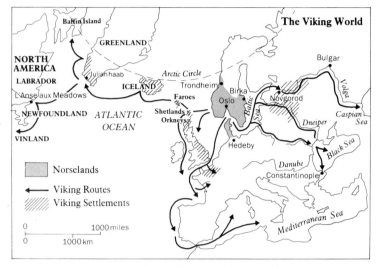

Map of the Viking world.

As mentioned before, the Vikings' home-lands were Norway, Sweden, and Denmark. Much of Norway is made up of fjords — valleys full of water that lead from deep in the mountains to the sea. There are many such fjords along the coast of Norway, some of them stretching over 100 miles.

A fjord has sides so steep that nobody can live on them. On the tops of the mountains, where some of the slopes are more gentle, farmers can graze a few animals. But this is possible only in the summer, since all through the winter the mountains are covered with snow.

As it is difficult to construct roads in Norway, people have always preferred to travel by boat along the fjords. Consequently, the Norwegian Vikings were exceptionally skillful boat builders and sailors.

Most of Norway lies as far north as Alaska, some of it being inside the Arctic Circle. Warm water from the Gulf Stream prevents the sea from freezing in winter, but the winters are very cold, especially up in the mountains, and also dark. Everywhere the days are very short, while in the far north the sun does not rise above the horizon for several weeks on end.

In the south of Norway there is some flat land which is suitable for farming. Unfortunately, there is not much of it.

Sweden, separated from Norway by a high range of mountains, is less rugged and spectacular. There are hills, woods, lakes, and marshes and, among them, patches of flat, fertile farmland. Along the coast are many deep bays and islands. As in Norway, the best way to travel in this country has always been by boat. The

Vikings from Sweden also made their living from the sea.

In Sweden, winters are even colder than in Norway, for the mountains stop warm air coming in from the Atlantic. Here, too, winter nights are very long, while in the north, weeks go by without any daylight at all. Toward the end of winter, villagers used to send scouts up into the hills. When they saw the sun rise for the first time, they ran down to report the exciting news.

Denmark is smaller than Norway or Sweden. In Viking times, however, it was richer and more powerful than either, because it is flat and has a lot of good farmland. The largest part of Denmark is Jutland, which is joined to the mainland of Europe. But the rest of Denmark is made up of about 500 islands, large and small. So the Danes, like their Scandinavian neighbors, have always relied on their boat builders and seamen.

Denmark, lying in the same latitude as the Alaskan panhandle and Scotland, has some daylight right through the winter. This season, nevertheless, is cold, especially when icy winds from Russia blow over the country.

THE THREE SONS OF RIG

Sogne Fjord, Norway. A typical fjord in which Norwegian Vikings would have built their boats.

The people who lived in the Viking lands had to be hardy, and some of the men were very tough indeed. Many tried to imitate the members of two semi-mythical groups, the Jomsvikings and the Berserks. The Jomsvikings were men between the ages of eighteen and fifty; their homes were fortresses where no women could enter, and they all lived by raiding and plundering. In battle, they defended one another like brothers, were never allowed to show fear, and, if they took booty, shared it equally.

The Berserks were even more fierce. Often they wore the skins of bears or wolves, and sometimes they went naked. They believed that the god Odin would save them from harm. In a fight, a Berserk would work himself into a terrible fury. He might even have a fit of rage when there were no enemies to kill and start wrestling with trees and large stones to stop himself from attacking his friends. If someone runs wild today, we may say, "He has gone berserk."

Not all Vikings were like the Jomsvikings and the Berserks. One can learn about ordinary Vikings from the legend of a god called Rig, who had three sons from three wives. The first son was named Thrall, which means "slave." He had an ugly face and a bent back, wrinkled skin on his hands and knobbly fingers. Thrall found himself a wife called Tir, who was just as ugly, with bow legs, scarred feet, and a hooked nose. Thrall and Tir had to do heavy, unpleasant work, such as mending fences, looking after pigs and goats, and spreading manure on the fields. Thrall and his family ate coarse bread, full of husks and cinders, for it was baked in hot ashes.

Rig's second son was named Karl, who was much better-looking than Thrall and did more skilled jobs. He built houses and barns, made carts, plowed the fields, and looked after the oxen and horses, considered to be nobler animals than pigs and goats. Karl's attractive wife wore a linen dress and carried the house keys on her belt. The family ate bread made from wheat, oats, and barley mixed together. Being baked on a hot stone, it was free from cinders.

Rig's third son was named Earl. He was tall, with blond hair and rosy cheeks, and his eyes were bright and fierce. Earl was good at war and at sports, for he could use a bow and arrow, throw a javelin, fight with a spear, ride, hunt, and swim. His wife was a beautiful princess. The family ate fine bread made only from wheat flour and baked on a bread iron.

The three sons of Rig described in the legend stand for the three main groups of people who lived in Viking lands: the slaves, the farmers, and the warriors.

CHAPTER 4

Valhalla and Ragnarok

The Vikings believed that the world was round and flat, like a pancake, with sea all along the edge. In the very middle was a tree called the World Tree. Its branches joined the earth to the heavens, while its roots joined the earth to the underworld. At the top of the tree, an eagle was perched, and at its foot, a snake lay coiled. The eagle and the snake were enemies. A little squirrel ran up and down the tree, carrying rude messages from one to the other.

The tree was in a city called Asgard, which was the home of twelve gods and twelve goddesses. The Vikings thought it was a real place, deep inside Russia, and explorers tried to find it. Around Asgard was a mighty wall that a giant had offered to build in a single winter. As payment, he demanded a beautiful goddess named Freyja. The gods agreed to his demands for they were sure the wall could never be finished in time. The giant, though, had a marvelous stallion to help him, and it was clear that the wall would soon be completed. However, a god called Loki turned himself into a mare and neighed at the stallion to lure him away from his work. The god Thor then killed the giant with his powerful hammer.

ODIN'S WARRIORS

At the gates of Asgard was a sentry called Heimdall, who was always on watch. Inside was a great hall known as Valhalla, the property of Odin. Valhalla had 140 doors, each door wide enough for 800 men to enter together. When a brave warrior died, he went to Valhalla, riding there on Odin's eight-legged horse, Sleipnir. On arrival, a beautiful girl called a Valkyrie greeted him with a cup of mead, an alcoholic drink made of honey and water.

Every morning, the warriors marched out of Valhalla. They spent the day fighting one another, but in the evening all the wounded were healed and all the dead brought back to life. They then spent the night feasting in Valhalla, waited on by Valkyries. They ate fresh pork from a pig that came back to life every time it was slaughtered, and they drank mead from horns which never ran dry.

Odin, who owned Valhalla, was the leader of the gods. The English called him "Woden," and he is still remembered today, for Wednesday is "Woden's day." Many Scandinavian kings claimed to be descended from him.

Odin was the god of war, who set kings fighting against one another and made warriors so wild with fury that they were afraid of nothing. The Berserks were his followers. Odin was also the god of those slain in battle, who lived in Valhalla. He was gathering an army, for he

12

Warriors feasting in Valhalla, the great hall of the god Odin, where Vikings went when they died.

knew that one day there would be a great battle that would herald the end of the world and the end of the gods.

In addition, Odin was the god of wisdom. One story is that he drank from a stream at the foot of the World Tree, and this made him wise, although he had to give an eye in payment. In Viking carvings he is usually shown with one eye. Another story is that he sacrificed himself to himself. He was pierced with a spear and hung from the World Tree for nine days and nine nights, during which time he had nothing to eat or drink. At the end of the nine days, he bent down and lifted some heavy stones carved with runes — the letters of the Viking alphabet. Thanks to their magic power he was freed from his suffering.

One of Odin's bravest warriors was Sigmund the Volsung. Odin gave him a magic sword, which would always bring him victory. Finally, however, the god fought against his hero, shattering the sword with his spear so that Sig-

mund was killed. Odin granted many victories to a king named Harald Wartooth, until there was a battle in which Odin, disguised as the driver of Harald's chariot, upset the vehicle, killing the king. Another great warrior killed by Odin after he had won many victories was Eric Blood-axe. When asked why he had permitted so brave a man to die, Odin replied, "The gray wolf is watching the home of the gods." He meant that he needed Eric for his army in Valhalla.

THOR'S HAMMER

A popular god with the Vikings was Thor, whose name is recalled in "Thursday," or "Thor's day." Thor, who was god of the sky, could cause a storm just by shaking his beard. As he rode through the heavens in a chariot drawn by two goats, lightning flashed, and thunder boomed. But Thor was friendly towards humans, for he could ward off plague and famine. Moreover, he fought monsters and giants who threatened

13

the earth. A poem written to Thor describes his victories over these enemies:

You broke Leikn's limbs,
You thrashed Thrivaldi,
You beat down Starkad,
You trampled on dead Gjalp,
Your hammer smashed Kella's skull,
You broke Kjallandi to bits.

Thor's weapon was a magic hammer which, if he threw it, always came back to his hand. Vikings often wore little charms in the shape of a hammer.

There are many stories about Thor. One tells of his attack on the World Serpent, which was a dangerous sea monster. Thor, disguised as a young man, visited a sea giant called Hymir, and offered to go fishing with him. Hymir sent Thor to find bait and, as they needed something large, Thor cut off the head of one of Hymir's oxen. The two then went to sea and

A twelfth-century Swedish tapestry showing three of the Viking gods. On the right, the one-eyed Odin carries an ax and a representation of the tree from which he hung; in the center, Thor carries his symbolic hammer; on the left, the fertility god Frey holds an ear of corn.

lowered their line. When the World Serpent took the bait, Thor pulled so hard on the line that his feet tore through the bottom of the boat, and he was left standing on the seabed. The head of the terrible monster rose above the waves, and Thor lifted his hammer to strike it. But Hymir was so terrified that he cut the fishing line, allowing the monster to escape.

Another story concerns a visit Thor made to Giant Land along with a young man named Thjalfi and the god Loki. On their way they came to a great hall which had a big opening down one side. They decided to sleep there. During the night, they heard a dreadful roaring, so Thor stood guard with his hammer until dawn. Then they saw a huge giant. The noise they had heard was his snoring, while the place they had assumed to be a hall was his glove.

The giant, whose name was Big Fellow, offered to go with them on their journey. That evening, Big Fellow told Thor to prepare supper, gave him a bag with some food in it, and went to sleep. Try as he might, Thor could not open the bag. In his anger, he hit Big Fellow on the head with his hammer, but the giant just opened an eye and asked if a leaf had fallen on him. They had to go without supper. During the night, Big Fellow snored again, keeping the others awake, so Thor hit him on the head a second time. The giant asked if he had been struck by an acorn. At dawn Thor gave the giant such a hard blow that the hammer smashed into his skull, but all the giant did was rub his eyes and wonder if a bird had dropped something on him.

Some days later, Thor and his friends reached Giant Land, where they took part in competitions. Thjalfi, a good runner, entered a race, but his rival beat him easily. Loki entered an eating contest, but even though he had a marvelous appetite, he, too, was beaten. Thor, a champion drinker, was given a horn to empty, but although he took three great draughts, it was as full as when he began. Thor then offered to wrestle with anyone and was amazed when an old woman came forward. He was even more amazed when she threw him to the ground.

The king of the giants then explained that Thor and his friends had been tricked by magic.

Big Fellow's head was a mountain, and although Thor had dented it with his hammer, he could not destroy it. Thjalfi's rival in the race was Thought, which moves far more swiftly than a human can run. Loki's opponent was Fire, which eats up all things even more quickly than a god can do. The tip of Thor's drinking horn was in the sea, which filled the horn as fast as the god drained it. And Thor's rival in the wrestling match was Old Age who, in the end, will overcome any person, however strong he or she may be.

MAGIC AND MISCHIEF

After Odin and Thor, the most important god was Frey, who was responsible for peace, plenty, animals, crops, and marriage, and whose emblem was a boar called Goldbristles. Frey could control the rain and the sunshine, which made him very important for farmers.

Two dwarfs had made Frey a magic ship. It was big enough to carry all the gods in Asgard, but, when not wanted, it could be folded small enough to go into a pouch. Frey had a twin sister named Freyja, the beautiful goddess whom the giant who built the wall around Asgard wanted as payment. When there was a war, people prayed to Odin; when there was a famine or plague, they called on Thor; when there was a marriage, they asked Frey to bless it.

The strangest of all the gods was Loki, who went with Thor to Giant Land. Some of the time he was friendly with the other gods, but more often he caused trouble.

After the pair of dwarfs had completed Frey's magic boat, Loki bet two other dwarfs that they could not make anything as wonderful, promising that if they succeeded, they could have his head. The dwarfs started to make a hammer for Thor. Loki turned himself into a fly, buzzing

A Viking charm in the shape of Thor's magic hammer.

around them as they worked and stinging one of them on the eye. As a result, the handle of the hammer was a bit too short, yet all the gods agreed, nonetheless, that the hammer was the most astonishing thing they had ever seen. The dwarfs immediately claimed Loki's head. Loki, however, protested that he had not offered his neck, and they must not touch it. Furious at being cheated, the dwarfs sewed up Loki's mouth.

Odin and his wife Frigg had a handsome son named Balder, whom everyone liked, except Loki. Frigg had received a promise from all plants, trees, and metals that nothing made from them would hurt her son.

The gods enjoyed throwing things at Balder, for they knew that any object that hit him would bounce off and do him no harm. But Frigg had forgotten to speak to the mistletoe. Loki made a dart from it, which he gave to Balder's brother, Holder, telling him to throw it at Balder, just for a joke. Holder did so, and Balder was killed.

Loki could turn himself into anything, male or female. As a female, Loki had some strange children. One was Sleipnir, Odin's eight-legged horse. Another was the goddess Hel, guardian of the underworld, who was half-black, half-white, and looked like a rotting corpse. Another was the World Serpent, which Thor had tried to catch. Yet another was the gray wolf, Fenrir, feared by Odin.

Fenrir lived just outside Asgard. He became so fierce that the gods decided to tie him up. Odin made a chain from the roots of a mountain, the noise of a meowing cat, and the breath of a fish. Although the chain was very strong, it looked like a slender cord of silk. Even so, Fenrir would not have it put on him unless someone placed a hand in his mouth. At last, the god Tyr agreed to do this, so Fenrir was tied up, even though Tyr lost his hand.

Thor fighting the World Serpent. An episode in the sequence of dramatic events culminating in the world's destruction and renewal.

DESTRUCTION AND NEW LIFE

The Vikings thought the world would end at a great battle known as Ragnarok, or the Doom of the Gods. Then, according to the legend, many strange and terrible events would take place in the world.

First, there would be a bitterly cold winter that lasted for three years. Then Fenrir, the wolf, would break loose, his open jaws stretching from earth to the heavens. At the same time, the World Serpent would rear above the sea and swim toward the shore, spitting poison. Along with the serpent would come a huge wave that would sweep over the land. On its crest would ride a ship, steered by Loki, and full of giants.

Then, at Asgard, the watchman Heimdall would sound his horn, whereupon Odin would lead his warriors from Valhalla toward a plain, where they planned to fight. Before the army got there, the wolf would seize Odin and devour him. Odin's son Vidar, who wore magic shoes, would place a foot on the wolf's lower jaw, grip the upper jaw with his hands, and tear the beast's head in two. Thor would struggle with the World Serpent and kill it but die from the poison it spat on him. Heimdall would fight with Loki. Odin's warriors would do battle against monsters and giants. In the end, everyone would be killed — gods, monsters, giants, and the whole human race.

The sea would then rise as high as the World Tree and flow back, leaving the earth clean, fresh, and pure. A new sun would shine in the sky, brighter than the older one, shedding a wonderful light on the mountains, where an eagle would appear. Within the World Tree would be two beings, Lif and Lifthrasir, and from them would come gods, people, and animals. It would be the beginning of new life in a new world.

CHAPTER 5

The Vikings at Home

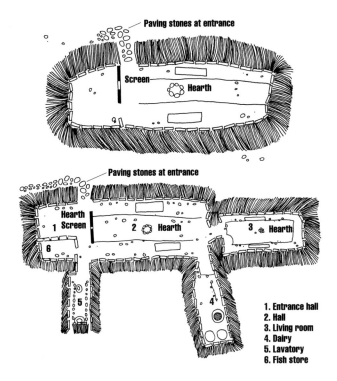

Most Vikings lived on farms. Although conditions were hard, they gradually improved their homes over the centuries.

The older type of Viking farmhouse, known as a "long house," was just one large room, or hall, where everyone lived, worked, ate, and slept. Down either side of the room were benches of earth edged with stone or wood. They were as high as the seat of a chair and about 6 feet (2 meters) wide. People sat on these benches during the day and slept on them at night. In the space between the benches was a stone hearth where the fire gave heat and light, and was used for cooking. If the weather allowed, the smoke escaped through a hole in the roof, but otherwise it just filled the room.

Sometimes the walls of the farmhouse were made of timber, but in most Viking countries this did not provide enough warmth so, instead, the people used earth faced with stone or turf. Earthen walls might be 6 feet (2 meters) thick to keep out the cold. Two rows of posts held up a roof of wooden rafters, covered with a thick layer of turf.

Apart from some paving stones near the door, the floor was of earth. It was strewn with rushes or straw for warmth, and this covering often concealed filth and debris, such as rotting pieces of food and the vomit of dogs and children.

There were no windows so that the only light came from the fire, the smoke hole in the roof, and little oil lamps. There was little or no ventilation either.

The house did not contain much furniture. There were tables, which were hauled up to the roof when they were not needed, chests for storing clothes, and shelves along some of the walls.

A Viking longhouse at top. This one is divided into two unequal parts by a screen. The smaller room might have been a store. Below, the plan of the farmhouse at Stong in Iceland.

SPACE AND COMFORT

Bit by bit the Vikings made their homes more comfortable. At Stong, in Iceland, is a larger and more advanced house, in which as many as twenty people may have lived. In some ways the Stong house was like the earlier kind, for it was built in the same way, with benches along the sides and a hearth in the middle of the hall. But there were important differences between the two houses.

The main thing is that the Stong house had three extra rooms: a toilet, a dairy, where cheese and butter were made, and a living room. The benches around the living room were too narrow for sleeping, so perhaps this was the dining room, while the fact that there was a loom in it shows that the women must have worked there. Inside the house, the walls were covered with wooden paneling which might be painted or carved.

The hall was divided unequally by a wooden screen, the smaller part making an entrance hall. In it was a place to store dry fish. The smells from that and the toilet must have been overpowering, so it is not surprising that, on some farms, the toilet was a separate building.

Near the farmhouse were other buildings, also of turf. There would be a barn, a pigsty, sheds for cows and goats, and perhaps a smithy. If the farm was near the coast, there would also be a shed with slatted sides, for drying fish.

Many farms had baths, which worked on the same principle as modern saunas. The people heated big stones in the fire, threw water on them, and then lay on benches in the steam. To improve their blood circulation, they beat themselves with bunches of twigs, and when they had finished, they went outside and jumped into cold water or rolled in the snow.

Viking farmhouse. The roof is made of turf, and goats feed on the grass.

THE FARMING YEAR

Farm work varied considerably in the different Viking lands. Because much of Denmark is flat and fertile, the people there could grow good crops. In many parts of Norway, however, farmers could grow very little, which meant they had to rely on animals. When Norwegians settled in Iceland, they raised both crops and animals. We know quite a lot about farms and farming in Iceland in Viking times.

An Icelandic farm had a large meadow near the house, with a wall around it to keep out animals. As the farmer put most of his manure on this meadow, it grew plenty of hay. Away from the house were other fields, some of them meadows, and others plowed for crops. Although these fields were protected by walls, the farmer could not spare much manure for them. Beyond the walled fields was open country where the animals wandered, finding any grass that they could.

The farmer's year began in the middle of April. The cows had stayed in their sheds all winter because of the cold, but now the snows had melted, and they could come out to graze.

From mid-April until mid-May was Cuckoo Month, or Sowing Time, when the arable fields were plowed and then sown with barley and oats.

From mid-May to mid-June was Egg Time. People scrambled about the cliffs and rocky islands where they collected some of the countless eggs laid by seabirds.

From mid-June to mid-July was Shieling Month, a "shieling" being a house in the mountains. Every farm had one. At this time of year the cattle were driven into the mountains to graze. Most of the farm people went with them and lived in their shieling where they spent their time milking the cows, sheep, and goats and turning the milk into butter and cheese.

Mid-July to mid-August was Haymaking Month when the grass was cut and hung on posts to dry before being carried to the farm on sledges. Here it was put in barns or made into ricks.

Mid-August to mid-September was Corn Cutting Month when the barley and oats were mown and carried into barns.

Mid-September to mid-October was Autumn Month. It was a busy time, for the sheep and cattle might have strayed for miles and had to be rounded up. The best ones were put in sheds and barns for the winter. Because there was not enough hay for the others, they were slaughtered, and the meat was salted.

Then the long winter began, although even in the short, dark days there was still work to do. The animals had to be fed and milked every day, while the biggest task was to thrash the grain. The people also mended their tools, their boats, and their buildings and tanned the skins of the animals they had killed. From the leather, they made harnesses, shoes, and clothing.

Most farmers kept slaves, who had to do the worst jobs. Some slaves were treated quite well. A Norwegian called Erling gave each of his slaves a number of tasks that lasted from one to three years, depending on how hard the slave worked. When the slave had finished, Erling set him free, gave him a plot of land, and taught him useful skills, such as how to catch herring. He also paid the man to work for him. But not all masters were like Erling. There was an Icelandic farmer who sometimes flew into terrible rages, and the only way he could calm himself was by killing one of his slaves.

FOOD AND DRINK

Since it was difficult to make a living by farming alone, the people had to do other things as well. It was noted earlier that one month of the year they gathered birds' eggs. They also went fishing, for which they used nets, lines, traps, and spears. Hunting often provided extra food and, moreover, some of the wild animals had valuable furs that were useful for trade. There was yet another way of making ends meet. This is what *The Saga of the Men of Orkney* tells us about a farmer called Sweyn:

Sweyn did much hard work in the spring, sowing a great deal of grain. When this work was over, he went raiding. He raided Scotland and Ireland until midsummer, which he called "spring raiding." He then stayed at home all

Viking kitchen utensils.

summer. When the crops had been reaped, he went raiding again and did not come back until one month of the winter was over. He called this "autumn raiding."

Viking farmers ate what they grew, gathered, or caught for themselves. There was nowhere to buy food, which meant that if the farmers

did not provide their own, they starved. Those whose farms were best situated grew a bigger variety of crops and enjoyed a better diet.

The Vikings' big problem was fresh meat. There was plenty in the autumn, when the weaker animals were slaughtered. Most of the meat, though, had to be salted. After a few months, it was not at all good to eat and, what is more, stocks might run out before the winter was over. One of the Viking ideas of heaven was to eat fresh pork every day.

The most common drink was beer, but the Vikings preferred mead, which was stronger. However, mead, like fresh pork, was a luxury — both were enjoyed regularly by the warriors in Valhalla — and seldom available to ordinary families.

The women cooked much of the food in cauldrons hung over the fire. Also, at the end of the hearth was a large, flat stone that could be heated and used for baking bread. Meat could be boiled in the cauldron, roasted on a spit, or put in a pit, a crude form of oven, along with some hot stones. The pit was covered with earth to keep in the heat.

Cauldrons were made of iron, while cooking

Cooking in a farmhouse. Note the many activities that are taking place in the one room.

pots were often made of soapstone. This stone, which is found in some parts of Norway, is easy to shape and is fireproof. The Vikings did not make pottery, so if a family owned any, it had either been bought or stolen in another country. Many kitchen utensils, such as scoops, ladles, buckets, barrels, and plates, were made from wood. Cutlery was knives, spoons, and fingers.

FAMILY LIFE

Viking women made all the clothes for their families. They spun and wove wool from their sheep and made linen cloth from flax. Their dyes came from colored rocks ground very fine, from plants, and even from some kinds of mud. To decorate their garments, they embroidered them and sewed on them narrow bands, woven in a special way to give complicated patterns. For ornament, they generally used colored wool, but if they were lucky, a trader called, bringing threads of silk or silver.

Men as well as women were fond of jewelry, boasting bracelets, neck bands, and necklaces. Brooches held their clothes together, so they were practical as well as beautiful. Also, a Viking woman had little chains hanging from one of her brooches on which she kept her keys, her comb, and her scissors. These are the sort of useful things a modern woman would put in her handbag.

A Viking family was more than parents and children, for it included grandparents, uncles, aunts, and cousins. The family usually stuck together. If any of its members was attacked, everyone would defend that person. If anybody was killed, they would take revenge by killing someone in the family of the murderer. As a result, blood feuds could start that might last for years. The only way to prevent such a feud was for the killer's family to pay a large sum of money to the victim's family.

When a baby was born, it was taken to the father. If it appeared weak or sickly, the father put it outside, where it was left to die. If the baby looked healthy, the father sprinkled it with water and gave it a name. Vikings did not have surnames as we do, but when they had grown up,

These brooches were worn by both men and women. Besides being ornamental, they fastened garments together.

many of them were given nicknames. We have already read about Olaf the Stout; others were Thorkel the Tall, Eric Bloodaxe, Harald Finehair, Olaf the Peacock, and Harald Bluetooth.

Children did not go to school but, instead, helped in the home and on the farm, learning what to do by copying the grown-ups. Children had to work hard, for no one liked a "charcoal chewer" — a boy or girl who wanted to sit by the fire and do nothing. By the time he was twelve, a boy was treated as a man. Olaf the Stout, for example, went on his first raid at that age.

In the summer there were outdoor games. The Vikings liked horse races, and they enjoyed watching horses fight, prodding the animals with pointed sticks to make them attack each other. There were athletics, too, most of which taught skills that might be useful in war. A swimming contest, for example, was not a race. You won if you held your opponent underwater until he collapsed.

During the winter evenings there were games to play indoors, but above all, the Vikings liked listening to the stories of their heroes. These sagas were told over and over again, so that everyone knew them by heart.

CHAPTER 6

Townsfolk and Traders

Although most Vikings lived on farms, some lived in towns. They built new towns or added to ones in all the countries where they settled.

It is clear, for example, that York, today a large city in the north of England, was formerly a Viking town, if only because of its street names. Many of these end in "gate," which comes from the Viking word "gata," meaning "street." Skeldergate is Shield Makers' Street; Coppergate is Cup Makers' Street; and Hungate is Dogs' Street.

Between 1976 and 1981, part of Viking York was excavated. The soil is damp, which keeps out the air. As a result, many things were preserved. There were the remains of buildings; there were boots, shoes, combs, pins, needles, and all sorts of household goods; and there were garbage dumps, which can reveal a great deal about how people lived. One of the most interesting finds was a set of panpipes, which still works. It plays five notes.

York stands on a neck of land at the meeting place of two rivers, the Ouse and the Foss, an easy position to defend. The Romans built a fortress here, and when they left, the Saxons occupied the town. The Vikings captured it in 866, renaming it Jorvik. They kept the fortress and also built a settlement outside it.

Jorvik grew to twice the size of the Saxon town. The Vikings made a new bridge over the Ouse River and built docks and warehouses, thus turning the place into a large port which traded with many other countries.

LIFE IN JORVIK

Four rows of houses were found in York. Some were built of wattle and daub. First, twigs were woven together to make something like a huge basket, and then a thick layer of clay was put on either side of it. The wattle kept the daub in place, on much the same principle as reinforcing in concrete. Other houses were made of sturdy oak planks. Roofs were covered with wooden shingles.

Each house was just one room about 24 feet (7.5 meters) long and 13 feet (4 meters) wide, the narrow end facing the street. As in a farmhouse, there was an earth bench for sitting and sleeping along each side of the room with a hearth in the middle. These rooms served for living, cooking, eating, and sleeping, but some were workshops as well. It is hard to imagine how all this activity could have gone on in such a small space.

One house belonged to a bone carver, who made combs, toggles, strap ends, game pieces, and skates. Another was the home of a woodworker who turned bowls, pots, and cups on his lathe. He also made buckets and barrels from wooden strips held together with hoops, a method that coopers still use today. Yet another house belonged to a jeweler. In addition to making things for sale, the people of Jorvik spun their own thread, wove their own cloth, and made their own clothes.

Behind each house was a small yard. In it was the outhouse, which was just a hole in the ground with a wooden seat over it. Garbage was thrown in the yard, where pigs, geese, and chickens scratched about in it. Jorvik was not a healthy place. Archaeologists have even found the remains of fleas and bugs that were alive in Viking times.

The garbage dumps reveal that the people ate bread made from wheat, oats, rye, and barley.

Blacksmith working at his forge. Making a good sword was a complicated, highly skilled, and almost magical process.

They also had beans, peas, apples, cherries, plums, and blackberries. Their favorite meat was beef, and they also had plenty of fish, for York is both on a river and near the coast. Most of the time they drank beer, but once in a while they enjoyed wine from the Rhineland.

Even though Jorvik was a town, its inhabitants had to grow most of their own food. There were fields just outside the town, where the people spent much of their time at farming or gardening.

THE VOYAGES OF OTTAR

In about the year 870, a Viking named Ottar came to England, bringing presents for Alfred the Great, king of the West Saxons. The conversations Ottar had with Alfred are written down, so we know a lot about him.

Ottar lived in the north of Norway, where he had a farm on which he kept cows, sheep, and pigs. He also owned a large herd of deer, well over 700 at any one time. The Saxon who wrote about him carefully explained that these deer

were called "reindeer," for he had never seen such animals himself. Ottar made most of his wealth from trade. He lived among a harmless, peaceful people known as the Lapps, and he took from them whatever he needed. This is what he told Alfred:

The Lapps pay me tribute. The tribute is animals' skins, feathers, walrus ivory, and ropes for ships. These ropes are made from the hides of walrus and seals. Every man pays according to his rank. An important man must pay fifteen marten skins, five walrus hides, one bearskin, ten bags of feathers, a tunic of bearskin, and two ropes. The ropes must be 60 ells long.

In the spring, Ottar loaded these goods into his ship and sailed south to Kaupang, a journey that took a month even if he had a following wind all the way. If the wind was against him, it took much longer. He was never far from land. Every night, he and his men went ashore and camped, for the coast of Norway is much too dangerous to navigate in the dark.

Kaupang was a small town with a good harbor, situated on the west side of Oslo Fjord. Its people smelted iron from which they made iron goods, and they also fashioned brooches and beads. In the summer, traders brought pottery from the Rhineland, glassware from France, and soapstone from other parts of Norway. Men like Ottar came from the far north, all bringing much the same goods as he did.

From Kaupang, Ottar sailed to Hedeby, a five-day voyage. Archaeologists have excavated Hedeby, which is on the Schlei Fjord, at the southern tip of the Jutland peninsula, in Denmark. Like York, it was built on damp ground that has preserved many of the things the Vikings left behind.

Hedeby had a sheltered harbor with docks and warehouses. As at York, some of the houses were of wattle and daub, and others of timber. Most of them were a little bigger than the York houses, being about 40 feet (12 meters) by 16 feet (5 meters). Moreover, each was divided into two or three rooms.

Many of the people of Hedeby, too, were craftsmen. They smelted iron from which they made weapons, cauldrons, knives, and tools. There were men who carved bone and ivory into combs, pins, knife and sword handles, and pieces for games. There were jewelers who cast and decorated beautiful bronze brooches and made beads from colored glass, amber, or pretty chips of rock.

The Hedeby townsfolk sold the objects they manufactured to traders, who, in return, brought goods from other lands. They were similar to those taken to Kaupang.

Viking merchants selling a slave to an Arab. Note the scales for weighing the purchase money.

ever heard, for they growl in their throats. It is worse than the howling of dogs.

SLAVES AND SILVER

The most valuable goods that the Vikings traded were slaves taken in raids on other countries. A few slaves were from Africa, but most were Europeans kept to work on their farms and some to be sold. Their best customers were the Arabs.

As long as the Vikings were pagans they took and sold slaves as they wanted. Later, when they became Christians, the church did not allow them to sell Christian slaves to the Arabs, who were Muslims, but they could sell pagan slaves to the Arabs and Christian slaves to other Christians.

What the Vikings wanted most from their trade was silver. Until the eleventh century they had no coins of their own, but other countries did. If a Viking was offered coins, he probably scratched or nicked them, to make sure they were silver all through, and then, instead of counting them, he weighed them. To make the exact weight he wanted, he might break a coin or chop off a piece of his bracelet. Viking hoards often contain broken coins and broken ornaments, which is called "hack silver." Every merchant carried a set of scales that could be folded neatly and put into a box or pouch. As we have seen, the Vikings buried their silver if they were afraid they might lose it, and, in modern times, many hoards have come to light.

Viking hack silver, one of the many hoards which have been excavated in modern times.

As Hedeby was the largest and richest of all the Viking towns, its inhabitants must have been proud of it. Others were not impressed. One of the traders who visited Hedeby was Ibrahim al-Tartushi, who came from Córdoba, a highly civilized Moorish city in southern Spain. This is what he said about Hedeby:

Its people worship Sirius. They hold a feast to honor their god and to eat and drink. When anyone sacrifices an animal to the god, he hangs it on a pole outside his door to show his neighbors he has made an offering to the god. The people have few goods or treasures. Their main food is fish, of which they have plenty. When a child is born, they often throw it into the sea to save the cost of keeping it. A woman can have a divorce whenever she wants. They wear eye makeup to make themselves beautiful. Their singing is the most dreadful I have

A set of weights which a Viking merchant would use to weigh his silver. Silver coins and bracelets were often broken to make the exact weight the merchant desired.

CHAPTER 7

Warriors and Warships

All Viking men knew how to fight, and each had his own weapons and armor. A rich man, dressed for battle, would wear a suit of chain mail, consisting of hundreds of little iron rings joined together. An ordinary soldier, however, could only afford a jacket of thick leather. The typical helmet was shaped like a cone with a piece sticking down in front to protect the man's nose. Vikings are sometimes drawn with horns on their helmets, but there is no evidence that they had these. The small round shield was made of wood, so it was fairly light, but in spite

A Viking warrior. His weapons are a sword and a spear. For protection, he has a helmet, a coat of chain mail, and a shield.

of its iron rim, it tended to split quite easily.

There were two kinds of spears. One was heavy for thrusting, and the other was light for throwing. Vikings spent a lot of time practicing their spear throwing. Some were strong and clever enough to throw two spears at a time, one with each hand; and a few could even catch an enemy's spear when it was in flight and hurl it back.

The battle-ax was a dangerous weapon. One type, the broadax, had a blade about one foot (30 centimeters) across. A man might wield his ax with both hands so as to deliver a mighty blow, but in order to do this, he had to sling his shield over his back. This was brave and risky, since he was now unprotected.

The Viking's favorite weapon was his sword. Swords were carefully made; they were strong and sharp, while their hilts were beautifully decorated with silver and copper. To harden them, the blades were heated red-hot and plunged into a liquid. The Vikings gave their swords names, such as "Gleam of Battle," "Serpent of the Wound," and "Fire of the Sea Kings."

A fight between two Vikings was as lively as a boxing match with the men jumping in all directions to dodge the blows. A Viking did not thrust with his sword, like a fencer, but swung it and hacked, hoping to split his enemy's skull or cut off an arm or leg. Meanwhile, he tried to parry his rival's sword with his shield.

During a battle, the men formed a solid mass. They advanced in "swine array," which meant that their line was a row of V's, like the teeth of a saw. The tip of each V was the "snout," and it was here that the Vikings put their best men. The snouts would force their way into an enemy army.

Buried Treasure

The Vikings had splendid ships. Several have been found, the most famous at Oseberg and Gokstad on the west side of Oslo Fjord. Both vessels had been used for burials, there being two women in the Oseberg ship and a man in the Gokstad ship. The ships and their contents were buried in blue clay, which kept out the air, thus preserving the wood from rotting. The Gokstad ship was discovered in 1880 and the Oseberg ship in 1904. After the vessels had been dug out of the ground, they were restored and are now in the Viking Ship Hall in Oslo, Norway.

Head of the Oseberg ship.

The Oseberg ship is beautifully carved, and many expensive goods were buried in it. Although not as strongly made as the Gokstad ship, it was very seaworthy, for in 1893 a Norwegian named Captain Magnus Anderson made a replica of it called the *Viking* and sailed it right across the Atlantic, from Norway to Newfoundland. The voyage took twenty-eight days.

The Gokstad ship is 76 feet (23.33 meters) long and 17 feet (5.25 meters) wide. Amidships, it is 6 feet (1.95 meters) deep. Fully laden, it could float in less than 3 feet (1 meter) of water. The keel — a single piece of oak — must have come from an enormous tree. At either end, the stem and stern post both rise up in graceful curves. Because their tips stuck out above the clay of the burial mound, the wood has rotted, but they were probably carved with the heads of fierce animals, some of which were found in the Oseberg ship. Most Viking ships were decorated with such heads, and some could be removed. Any ship bound for Iceland had to take down its figureheads, in case they frightened the good spirits on shore.

The planks that make the sides of the ship are fixed to the ribs. Above the waterline, this is done with wooden pegs, but below the waterline, the planks are tied to the ribs with the roots of spruce trees. Ties such as this made the ship flexible so that when a wave hit it, it would give just a little and be less likely to break in a storm. Captain Anderson's *Viking* would sometimes twist about 6 inches (15 centimeters) out of alignment.

The oar-shaped rudder is on the ship's side. In order for it to be effective, it went well down into the water, below the keel. If the water was shallow, the rudder could be swung up to keep it from hitting the bottom.

On either side of the Gokstad ship are sixteen holes for oars. There are no benches for rowers, which is a puzzle, although perhaps the men sat on their sea chests.

Along the side of the ship is a rail from which shields were hung, thirty-two on each side. Half were painted black and half yellow, and they were put up alternately all around the ship. Probably, the shields were just for show, when

The Gokstad ship being excavated in 1880. The ship was in remarkably good condition considering it had lain in the ground since the year A.D. 850.

Viking ship under sail. Such ships are often depicted with shields along the side but, probably, they were only carried for ornament when in harbor.

the ship was in harbor, since they would have been in the way at sea.

Part of the mast has rotted, although it may have been 40 feet (12 meters) high. We know from stone carvings that the sails of Viking ships were roughly square, while the sagas say they were made of wide strips of different colors.

In the ship were cooking utensils, like those on a farm. The men could only light a fire on shore, so on a long sea journey they had to eat uncooked food, which might be dried fish, smoked meat, cheese, and nuts.

The Oseberg ship has a wooden frame for a tent that the crew could pitch on the ship or on land. The men had sleeping bags made from animal skins.

BRAVING THE SEAS

A long voyage in the Gokstad ship must have been an ordeal. The little vessel probably rode the waves well but was tossed up and down. The men had no hot food or hot drink and no warm cabin for shelter against rain, sleet, snow, and continual spray from the sea.

The Gokstad ship was built in about 850. In later years the Vikings built larger ships, one of the biggest being the *Long Serpent,* which belonged to King Olaf Tryggvason of Norway. This vessel had thirty-four pairs of oars and was 120 feet (37 meters) long, while the Gokstad ship had only sixteen pairs of oars and was 76 feet (23 meters) long. According to one of the sagas, the *Long Serpent* could carry 574 men, although 200 seems more likely.

A Viking was proud of his ship. He called it his "surf dragon," his "horse of the breakers," or his "oar-steed."

Vessels like the Gokstad ship were perfect for raiding. They were fast and had oars and sails so that the Vikings could make a surprise attack wherever they wanted. They could leave as quickly as they came. They had no problems with landing, since they just ran their ships onto the beach and jumped ashore. If need be, they could row a long way up the river, deep into enemy country.

28

CHAPTER 8

The Vikings Attack England

Ruins of the Abbey and Castle of Lindisfarne in the northeast of England, the site of one of the earliest Viking raids on the British Isles.

One day in 789, men from three ships landed on the Dorset coast of England, near Portland. The reeve of Dorchester, who was the king's local official, went to find out who these strangers were. As soon as he arrived, they killed him.

Four years later, in 793, there was an attack on the island of Lindisfarne, where the only inhabitants were monks. Ships were run onto the beach, and armed men leaped ashore. The *Anglo-Saxon Chronicle* describes what they did:

> They lay waste everything in sight. They trample the holy relics under foot. They throw down the altars. They seize the treasure of the holy church. Some of the monks they kill outright. Others they carry away with them. A great many they insult and beat and fling out naked. Others they drown in the sea. Then they depart, boasting about their plunder and their wicked deeds.

These were the first Viking attacks on England, attacks that were to go on for nearly 300 years. Nor was England the only country to suffer, for the Vikings raided many other coasts of Europe.

ADVENTURE AND WEALTH

There were many reasons why the Vikings went raiding, some of which can be deduced from the extract in the *Anglo-Saxon Chronicle*. In the first place, it is clear that the Vikings liked excitement. They took pleasure in causing damage and they saw nothing wrong in robbing and killing foreigners. The god Odin encouraged them to do battle, and the Viking idea of heaven was to spend every day fighting. Next, the *Anglo-Saxon Chronicle* says that the Vikings carried away church treasures. Thirdly, reports the *Chronicle*, the Vikings took captive some of the monks, who would have been sold as slaves. Here, then,

Map of Saxon England.

are three reasons why the Vikings went off on raids. They sought adventure, plunder, and slaves.

A further reason is that, as stated earlier, life in Scandinavia was difficult. People could just make a living by farming and trading, but both involved hard work, and less effort was needed to go raiding. With any luck, they might find a rich monastery to plunder, but if not, they could always kidnap some prisoners to sell in the slave market.

RAIDERS AND SETTLERS

Most of the early Viking attacks on England were hit-and-run raids by Danes. A few ships would land at a place that was easy to defend, such as an island in a river. Then, while some of the men guarded the ships, the others found themselves horses to ride around the countryside. They stole anything that was worth taking, burned villages, and killed invalids, old people, and children. They put the younger men and women in chains and led them back to the ships. Then they sailed away before an English army had time to reach the spot.

Later, fleets of many Danish ships arrived, carrying whole armies. These were in no hurry to leave but would fight a battle if they were attacked.

Worse was to follow, for the Danes came, not just to raid, but to settle for good. It began with the capture of York in 865. There is a strange story about this. King Aella of Northumbria caught a Danish leader called Ragnar Hairy-Breeches and put him in a snake pit. As he was dying, Ragnar called out, "How the piglets would grunt if they knew what was happening to the boar!" By the boar, he meant himself, while the piglets were his two sons, Ivan the Boneless and Halfdan of the Wide Embrace. When they heard what had happened to Ragnar, they invaded Northumbria, capturing both York and King Aella. As their revenge, they broke open his ribs and tore out his lungs.

This story may or may not be true, but a Danish army certainly did take York and then settled in northern England. They brought over their families and began farming and trading.

Next, the Danes invaded East Anglia and killed its king, Edmund. According to one legend, they tied him to a tree and shot him full of arrows. Edmund became a saint, and a monastery was named after him.

The third part of the country to fall was Mercia in central England. The Danes conquered most of the area in 873.

The first Viking landing in England on the Dorset coast. The Saxon official, on the horse, is asking the Vikings what they are doing. Their answer was to kill him.

Vikings sack a Saxon village. They would kill the old people but take the young as slaves.

ALFRED RESISTS THE DANES

Now the only Saxon kingdom left was Wessex. A Danish army under King Guthrum had already attacked it in 871, but it was bravely defended by King Ethelred and his younger brother, Alfred. There were various battles, some won by the Danes, some by the Saxons. Before the year ended, Ethelred died, and Alfred, aged only twenty-two, became king. He persuaded Guthrum to make peace by paying him a large sum of money.

Guthrum attacked Wessex again in 876. He failed, however, to defeat Alfred, partly because he lost many of his ships during a storm off the coast of Dorset, near Swanage.

In 878 Alfred was spending Christmas at Chippenham in Wiltshire, when Guthrum launched his third attack. Alfred was taken by surprise, since it was most unusual for an army to fight during the winter. The Saxons were defeated, and Alfred had to flee to the island of Athelney, in the nearby Somerset marshes.

It is said that after the Battle of Chippenham, Alfred took refuge in a peasant's hut. As neither the man nor his wife knew who he was, they gave him jobs to do. One was to watch some cakes that were baking, but Alfred was so busy worrying about the Danes that he let the cakes burn. The peasant's wife gave him a scolding. This story may not be true, for it was not written down until 150 years after Alfred's death. And if the king did burn anything, it was bread, for Saxon peasants did not have cakes.

effective, and the Saxons did not win many battles at sea.

Alfred had more success on land. It had always been a problem to make his men leave their farms to fight, because in those days people had to grow all their own food, and if they missed seed time or harvest, they risked dying of starvation. Alfred solved this problem by calling out only half of his men at a time. They then took turns, one half farming while the other was fighting.

Alfred also built strong walls around many of his towns. These fortified places were called "burghs." There were never more than twenty miles between one burgh and the next, and every family had to send a man to defend the one nearest to it. The Danes had much more difficulty invading Wessex, now that it contained so many fortresses.

Alfred died in 899, fighting the Danes until the very end. He was never able to stop their attacks, but he had saved much of England from them.

On Alfred's death, his son Edward was crowned king of Wessex. Alfred's daughter Ethelflead had married the king of Mercia, and when he died, she ruled Mercia, becoming the only woman ever to govern a Saxon kingdom. Brother and sister attacked the Danelaw, winning back all of England as far north as the Humber River. When Edward died, his son Athelstan conquered the rest of the country. The Danes who had settled in England kept their homes, but they were now under the rule of a Saxon king.

Alfred stayed in hiding until the spring and then, after the crops had been sown, he gathered an army. There was a great battle at Edington, near Chippenham. The Danes were defeated and fled into the town where, after a siege of two weeks, they surrendered.

A DIVIDED LAND

In 885 Alfred made a treaty with Guthrum whereby the two leaders agreed on a frontier. South of the line was Alfred's kingdom of Wessex and its ally, the kingdom of Mercia. The lands north of the line, known as the "Danelaw," belonged to Guthrum and other Danish rulers.

Alfred's troubles did not end with the defeat of Guthrum, for more Danish armies attacked Wessex and were often assisted by the Danes in East Anglia, in spite of their promise. Alfred, however, found new ways of dealing with the Danes. He built a fleet — the first true English navy. But although his ships were bigger than those of the Danes, in many ways they were less

CHAPTER 9

A Danish King of England

In 978 the king of England was a young man named Edward. One day, while hunting in Dorset, he found himself near Corfe, where there was a hunting lodge. He knew that his step-mother Ethelfrith and his half brother Ethelred were staying there, so he called to see them. When he rode up to the gate, a servant came out and handed him a cup of wine, but as Edward bent forward to take it, another servant stabbed him in the back. The horse ran off, dragging Edward along the ground. When they picked Edward up, he was dead.

It is not certain whether Ethelfrith ordered the murder, but a month later her own son, Ethelred II, was crowned king. He was only ten, and he reigned for forty years. This was a bad time for England, for the Vikings now began a new kind of raid. The first Vikings to arrive had been looking for treasure and slaves; later, they settled in England to become farmers and traders. However, the Vikings who came in the time of Ethelred II wanted huge sums of the protection money known as danegeld. Large armies invaded England to storm up and down the country, burning and killing. Then they offered to leave, if they were given thousands of pounds of silver. The English nearly always paid, but within a few years the Vikings returned, demanding even more silver. For various reasons, the English were powerless to stop these attacks.

MUDDLE AND MASSACRE

When Ethelred II grew up, he proved a bad king. His people called him "unraed," so he has become known as "Ethelred the Unready," although a more accurate meaning for "unraed"

is "unwise." Worse still, Ethelred was treacherous and cruel. He and his nobles did not trust one another, as just one story will show. When Ethelred II laid a trap for a Danish fleet, a Saxon nobleman named Aelfric warned it. In revenge, Ethelred had Aelfric's son blinded.

Ethelred II was an exceptionally poor leader, hardly ever sending his soldiers to the right place. The *Anglo-Saxon Chronicle* says, "When the enemy was in the east, our army was in the

Murder of King Edward at Corfe in Dorset.

The Battle of Maldon in A.D. 991 resulted in a Viking victory over the Saxons.

west. When the enemy was in the south, our army was in the north." The Viking armies were now larger than they had ever been, and the many Danes living in England helped the invaders.

The first big Viking attack of Ethelred's reign was in 991. It was led by the king of Norway, Olaf Tryggvason. His army camped on Northey Island, near Maldon in Essex. A Saxon army marched there to give battle. Joining the island to the mainland is a narrow causeway which the Vikings could only cross a few at a time, and as fast as they did so, the Saxons killed them. The Vikings protested. "Let us across," they shouted, "and give us a fair fight." Foolishly, the Saxons agreed and fell back from the causeway. The Vikings swarmed over it, defeated the Saxons, and killed their leader. Soon after the Battle of Maldon, King Ethelred gave Olaf Tryggvason 22,000 pounds of silver to go away.

In 994 Olaf returned, along with King Sweyn Forkbeard of Denmark. After they had done considerable damage, Ethelred paid them 16,000 pounds of silver. Between 997 and 1001 the Vikings attacked England repeatedly until, in the end, Ethelred paid them 24,000 additional pounds of silver. The Vikings promised not to return and gave Ethelred some hostages, including Gunnhild, the sister of Sweyn Forkbeard.

Ethelred knew that the Vikings would not keep their promise and became so desperate that he decided to kill all the Danes living in England. The massacre occurred in 1002, on November 13, St. Brice's Day. The Saxons killed without mercy, burying some of the adults alive and violently murdering children. Hundreds of Danes died, among them Gunnhild. Sweyn was furious. He led an army into the heart of England and won a great battle at Avebury, in Wiltshire. Ethelred had to pay him 36,000 pounds of silver as danegeld.

There are two famous legends from these wars. One is about daneskins. If ever the Saxons caught a Dane, so it was said, they peeled off his skin while he was still alive and nailed it on their church door. Scraps of skin have indeed been found on some Saxon church doors. Scientists have examined them, and most seem to be cowhide; but pieces at Copford and Hadstock in Essex might, possibly, be human skin.

The other legend concerns a Viking attack on London Bridge, led by Olaf the Stout, later St. Olaf. In those days London Bridge was built of wood. Olaf's men sailed up to the bridge carrying hooks on the ends of ropes, flung the hooks onto the bridge, and rowed with all their might until the bridge collapsed. This story might explain the origins of the nursery rhyme *London Bridge Is Falling Down*. Some grappling irons have been found in the Thames River, so the tale might just be true.

CANUTE BRINGS PEACE

In 1013 Sweyn Forkbeard decided to conquer England. He and his son Canute arrived with a large army, attacking so fiercely that Ethelred fled to France. The next year, however, Sweyn died. Canute was only eighteen and not sure he could continue the war, he went back to Denmark.

In 1015 Canute returned. By now the Saxons had found an able leader, Ethelred's son, Edmund Ironside. Under him, the Saxons fought bravely, winning as many battles as they lost. In the end, Canute agreed to make peace, and he and Edmund divided England between them.

Suddenly, in 1016, Edmund died. The Saxon nobles now chose Canute as their king. This may seem a strange thing to do, but the Saxons, tired of war, wanted a strong leader who would keep their enemies at bay. There was one last danegeld to pay, the largest of all. Canute took 82,500 pounds of silver which he shared among his Danish troops before sending them home.

Canute was already king of Denmark, and in 1028 he also took Norway from Olaf the Stout. With the addition of England, he was now monarch of a large empire, surrounding the North Sea. Canute ruled well. Even though he had two wives, he was a Christian. He built churches and monasteries. Much more importantly, he prevented other Vikings from attacking England.

An English monk named Henry of Huntington wrote a strange story about Canute. The king ordered his throne to be placed on a beach at low tide and then called to the waves, "This land is mine. No one has ever disobeyed me. I forbid you to invade my land and make my feet wet." Of course, the tide rushed in, and Canute had wet feet and wet legs as well. Often, this is as much of the story as is told, making the king look foolish, but Henry of Huntington completed it with a moral. Canute jumped back to dry land and remarked to his courtiers, "You can see that kings really have no power. All power belongs to God." He then took off his crown and never wore it again.

Canute died in 1035 and his son Hardecanute ruled England. When he also died, the Saxons chose Edward, another son of Ethelred II, to be their king. Edward was called "the Confessor," because he was very religious, but he was no soldier. The English were fortunate since, for most of Edward's reign, the Vikings were too busy fighting each other elsewhere.

The massacre of St. Brice's Day, A.D. 1002, Ethelred's revenge on the Vikings.

CHAPTER 10

The Vikings in Ireland, France, and Italy

The first Vikings to attack Ireland were Norwegians, who sailed there around the north of Scotland. The earliest recorded raid was in 795, only two years after the attack on Lindisfarne. Here, too, the Vikings plundered monasteries and took slaves, making the Irish long for bad weather so that the Vikings could not land. In the margin of a book he was copying, one monk wrote:

Bitter is the wind tonight,
White the foam on the sea.
I have no fear the Viking hordes
Will sail the sea on such a night.

The Vikings found it easy to raid Ireland, for the country was divided. There was a high king, but he had no power over the Irish tribes, who were always stealing one another's cattle and fighting. In 807 there was even a battle between the monks of two monasteries, Cork and Clonfert.

Head of an Irish crozier, dating from the time of the Viking assaults on Ireland.

THE BATTLES FOR IRELAND

The Viking assaults on Ireland became more and more dangerous. The leader most hated by the Irish was Sturgeis, who caused terrible damage for about seven years. An Irish chronicle reports that when he sacked the monastery of Clonmacnoise, he stood his wife on the high altar, where she chanted heathen spells and curses.

There is a legend that a beautiful Irish princess trapped Sturgeis. She pretended to be in love with him and asked him to meet her in secret, but her "maids" turned out to be armed men in disguise. They captured Sturgeis and drowned him.

The Irish called the Norwegians "white strangers." In 852 bands of Danes whom the Irish called "black strangers," invaded. There was now terrible confusion, for the Danes fought with the Norwegians, and the Irish fought with both. Some Vikings were even willing to side with the Irish, provided they were paid.

There was one great battle against the Norwegians that Orm, the Danish leader, seemed likely to lose. So, even though he was a pagan, he called on St. Patrick for help and won a victory. The Norwegians had stolen a chest of treasure from St. Patrick's shrine, which Orm returned in gratitude to the saint.

The Danes made piles of the Norwegian dead and lit fires so that the bodies swelled and burst. When the Irish protested, the Danes merely pointed out that the Norwegians would have done the same to them had they won.

Orm's victory was wasted for, in 853, the Norwegians drove the Danes from Ireland and eventually settled there. Vikings from Ireland also made homes on the Isle of Man, and in northwest England and southwest Scotland. There are many Viking remains on the Isle of Man, including some interesting crosses that have both pagan and Christian figures carved on them.

Viking fleet in river. The ships drew little water, so they could be rowed a long way up rivers and far into enemy territory.

In 1014 an Irish leader named Brian Boru decided he would attack the king of Dublin, Sigtrygg Silky Beard, and both sides gathered an army. Two Viking chiefs, Brodir and Ospak, came from the Isle of Man to help Sigtrygg. There was a great battle at Clontarf. Ospak heard a prophecy that the Vikings would be defeated, so he switched sides and fought for the Irish.

Brian Boru kept out of the battle. He had two excuses, the first being that he was old and the second that it was Good Friday, and he considered it wrong to fight on such a holy day. Sigtrygg also avoided the battle, for which he had no excuse at all.

The Irish won the Battle of Clontarf. As Brodir was running away, he saw Brian Boru sitting under a tree and killed him. At once, the Irish seized Brodir. They dragged him around and around the tree, cutting open his stomach and tearing out his intestines.

After Clontarf, the Vikings who were in Ireland remained there. Now, however, they came under the rule of the Irish.

TERROR BY RIVER

Another country that the Vikings found easy to attack was France. The French were constantly squabbling among themselves, their king had little power, and the Vikings could sail up the wide, long rivers right into the heart of the land.

France A.D. 800

Map of France.

There were now Viking attacks all over France. A monk wrote:

> The number of ships grows. The flood of Vikings never stops. Everywhere they kill, burn, and plunder. No one can stop them. They seize the cities of Bordeaux, Limoges, Angoulême, and Toulouse. They turn Angers, Tours, and Orléans into deserts. They carry off the holy relics of many saints.
>
> Ships without number voyage up the Seine. Rouen is burnt. Paris, Beauvais, and Meaux are captured. The fortress of Melun is destroyed. Chartres, Evreux, and Bayeux are looted and every town is besieged.

The French, though, did fight back, and when the Vikings attacked Paris in 885, they received a shock. The old town of Paris stood on an island in the Seine River, with two bridges joining it to

In 841 the Vikings ventured up the Seine River and sacked Rouen. They laid waste to the country around it, burning farms, villages, and monasteries.

The next year the invaders sailed up the Loire to Nantes. It was St. John's Day, June 24, which was a holiday, so the town was crowded. When the Vikings burst into Nantes, many people took refuge in the cathedral, but the Vikings slaughtered them all, including the bishop. They then rampaged through the streets, burning and killing until, finally, they left, carrying slaves and plunder with them. A French baron, who had helped the Vikings capture Nantes, kept the town for himself when they had departed.

In 845 a Viking named Ragnar led a fleet of 120 ships again up the Seine. To check the enemy advance, the French king, Charles the Bald, positioned part of his army on one side of the river and part on the other. This was a mistake. Ragnar and his men defeated the smaller French force quite easily and then hanged 111 prisoners in full view of the rest, who were so frightened that they fled. Charles paid Ragnar 7,000 pounds of silver to go away.

the mainland, one to the north and the other to the south. The citizens had fortified these bridges so that the Vikings could not sail past them.

First of all, the Vikings attacked the bridges from their ships, but the defenders shot arrows, threw stones, and poured down boiling water and boiling oil. Screaming Vikings jumped into the river to cool themselves. The Vikings then attacked from the land. They made huge battering rams, protected by wooden screens, but boiling oil burned the shelters and scalded the men inside them. Next, the Vikings set some of their own ships on fire and propelled them toward the bridges, but the flames did no damage to the stone arches. Finally, the Vikings tried a kind of germ warfare. They killed oxen and prisoners and flung the bodies into the ditch that ran around the town, hoping that as the corpses rotted, they would spread disease among the defenders. That did not work either.

The siege lasted for eleven months until, in the end, the French king, Charles the Fat, ar-

rived with an army. He drove the Vikings from Paris and allowed them to escape to Burgundy, in eastern France. He also promised them 700 pounds of silver. The people of Burgundy were in rebellion, and by sending the Vikings against them, he saved himself a lot of trouble. The following year, the Vikings returned to Paris, demanding their payment of silver, but the citizens chased them away.

ROLF THE GANGER

Early in the tenth century, a band of Danish Vikings conquered some land around the mouth of the Seine. Their leader was called Rolf, a huge man whose legs were so long that his feet trailed on the ground if he tried to ride a horse. So, because he had to go everywhere on foot, he was known as "Rolf the Ganger" ("walker").

At that time, the king of France was yet another Charles, nicknamed the "Simple," although, in fact, he was far from stupid. In 911

The people of Paris defend their bridge against the Vikings. The town was besieged for almost a year and eventually relieved by the army of Charles the Fat.

Charles beat Rolf in a battle which, as he realized, gave him a good opportunity. He made a treaty by which Rolf was to keep all of the lands he had taken near the mouth of the Seine and, in return, was to become a Christian and swear homage to Charles. Most important of all, he was to prevent other Vikings from sailing up the Seine to attack France.

Once he had been baptized, Rolf came to swear homage to Charles, which meant he would have to kiss the king's feet. Rolf was a proud man and did not like the idea, but he knew he must keep his word. When the moment came, he seized Charles by the ankles, lifted him into the air and kissed his feet while holding him upside down.

For a time, it seemed that Charles had made a good bargain, for Rolf certainly kept out the other Vikings. But he also took more and more of France for himself, and his descendants did the same until their lands became the great duchy of Normandy. In the end a duke of Normandy conquered England, making himself more powerful than the king of France.

IN SEARCH OF ROME

In 857 some Vikings under Bjorn Ironside had ransacked Paris. Encouraged by his success, Bjorn decided to go one better. He would sack Rome, the greatest city in Europe. He and his friend Hastein set sail with a fleet. They were to be away for four years. On their way, they attacked Spain, which was a mistake, for Spain in those days was ruled by Arabs, who were better at war than the Vikings. Ironside and Hastein fled, having lost two ships. Then, after raiding the south of France, they worked their way down the coast of Italy. Soon, they came to a large city built of white marble which they were sure was Rome.

The city had such strong walls that the Vikings did not think they could storm them. Instead, they attempted a trick. Hastein pretended to be ill, and the Vikings sent a message to the town saying that their leader was dying and wished to be baptized. A priest came out to perform the ceremony. Next day, the Vikings said their leader was dead and asked if he could be buried in the cathedral. Again, the citizens agreed. Just as the coffin was being lowered into the ground, Hastein jumped out of it. He killed the bishop who was conducting the service and, at the same time, his Viking companions drew the swords they had hidden. They fought their way to the gates and opened them for the rest of the army.

Ironside and Hastein now found that they were nowhere near Rome but at a town called Luna. They were so enraged that they destroyed the place completely.

This is a saga story that may well be fiction. Luna is now called Luni. It has been excavated, but there is no sign that it was destroyed during the period of the Vikings.

Not many other Vikings followed Ironside and Hastein into the Mediterranean, because the Arabs were very powerful in North Africa and Spain. The Arabs were great pirates themselves, and they knew how to deal with Vikings.

Hastein surprises the bishop of Luna.

CHAPTER 11

The Way to America

It is most likely that the Vikings reached America in about A.D. 1000, almost 500 years before Columbus. The Vikings, however, did not sail to America in a single voyage but went by stages, so that it took them almost 200 years.

First of all, some Norwegians settled in the Orkney, Shetland, and Faroe Islands. This may have been in the ninth century, although it could have been earlier. The settlers lived by farming, fishing, seal hunting, and trade, and they also went raiding, particularly in Ireland.

Next, the Vikings journeyed to Iceland. Nearly all of the country was covered with ice and snow. Moreover, there were volcanoes. Every five years or so one of them would erupt, or there would be an earthquake. But around the coast there was a belt of land that was free from snow and ice. Much of it was good for farming. Also, the sea was full of fish.

The Vikings were not the first people to reach Iceland, for some Irish monks had sailed there, hoping to live in peace. They were amazed to find that the sun hardly set in midsummer, and one said that even at midnight he could see well enough to pick lice out of his clothes. The monks left in a hurry when those unwelcome visitors, the Vikings, arrived.

The first Vikings to see Iceland were sailors who reached it by accident, having been lost in a fog or, perhaps, blown off course in a storm. They told others what they had found.

A FERTILE LAND

In 860 a Norwegian named Floki decided to settle in this strange new land. He went first to the Faroe Islands and knew he had to sail north-

Floki releases a raven. If the bird sees land, it will fly to it, thus showing Floki the direction he should sail.

west from there but not how far. He was accompanied by some unwilling passengers — three ravens, who were longing for dry land. He let the first go, and it came back to the ship. Later, he released the second bird, but it, too, returned to the ship. When the third raven failed to fly back, however, Floki realized it was a good sign, so he sailed in the same direction taken by the bird. Sure enough, he discovered land. After that, Floki received the nickname "Ravens."

Floki and his people had brought animals with them, and they also had grain to sow; but they found so many fish that they spent all their time catching them and neglected their farming. The winter was so terrible that the settlers nearly died of starvation. They decided to leave but, before they did so, "Ravens" Floki climbed a hill and, having looked with dismay at all the glaciers, named the country "Iceland." One of his Vikings, Thorolf, was not so discouraged. He said butter dripped from every blade of grass, meaning that it was a good place for cattle. For that, they called him "Thorolf Butter."

It was some years before other Vikings sailed to Iceland. Then, in 874, two brothers called Ingolf and Leif went raiding. They quarreled with some young noblemen in their party, and Leif killed two of them. After that, they dared not return home, so they settled a safe distance away, in Iceland. Before they went, Leif raided Ireland, where he captured some slaves to do the hard work when they reached their new home.

Ingolf had two wooden columns with him, carved with images of gods and sacred objects. He threw them into the sea and waited until they drifted ashore. After three years, he found the columns. They were close to what is now Reykjaviik, the capital of Iceland, and it was here that Ingolf built his farm. Leif settled somewhere else, not bothering with sacred columns. That may have been shortsighted, because, before long, his Irish slaves killed him and carried off his womenfolk.

Vikings from western Norway now flocked to Iceland. According to the sagas, this was because King Harald Finehair was trying to bring all Norway under his rule, and people wanted to escape from him. More probably, they were looking for good farmland, which was so scarce at home.

One of the new arrivals, a man named Scallagrim, chose his farm in much the same way as Ingolf had done, but it was not wooden columns that he floated ashore. It was his father's coffin.

The first colonists took all the land they wanted, although it soon had to be rationed. Each man and woman was allotted as much as they could walk around in a day, he carrying a fire, she leading a cow. Even then, these were still large farms.

ERIC THE RED

One Norwegian who went to Iceland was named Eric the Red, who, so the sagas relate, had left Norway "because of some killing." He was soon in trouble in Iceland, being that sort of man. He quarreled with a neighbor over nothing more serious than the loan of some benches, and there was a fight in which seven men were killed. Eric was banished for three years.

Eric knew there was land to the west of Iceland, since a few Vikings had already tried to

Sailing the Atlantic. These merchant ships, called "knorrs," were tubbier than warships, so they could carry cargo and livestock.

settle there. After some had died of starvation, and some had fought and killed each other, the survivors came home. Eric spent his three years of exile exploring this country. He found that it was like Iceland, most of it being covered with glaciers but with good farmland near the coast. Eric decided to settle there and, to tempt people to join him, he advertised it as "Greenland."

Plenty of Icelanders were eager to go with Eric, which may seem surprising, but they were escaping from famine at home. A saga describes it:

Men ate ravens and foxes. Many horrible things were eaten which should not have been. Some men had the old and helpless put to death and thrown over cliffs. Many starved to death. Others stole and were killed for it. Even outlaws killed each other.

Eric and his followers set sail in 896. They had twenty-five ships, but because of a storm, only fourteen arrived, which gives some idea of the perils the Vikings faced on their voyages.

Eric settled on the southwestern tip of Greenland, near what is now Julianehaab, where he built a farm that he called Brattahlid, or Hill Farm. Later, much to Eric's disgust, his wife became a Christian and refused to stay with him. She built a little church but put it up just out of sight of the farm, so as not to annoy her husband.

Many of Eric's followers traveled 300 miles up the west coast of Greenland to Godthaab. Perhaps they wanted to be safely away from Eric!

Other settlers came from Iceland. Archaeologists have found 350 Viking farms in Greenland, which suggests the population may have numbered about 3,000. The Vikings found native people in Greenland and called them "Skraelings" or savages, today's Inuit or Eskimos. We do not know how the Vikings treated the natives but, as a rule, they robbed and killed people who could not defend themselves.

SAILING THE ATLANTIC

For their Atlantic voyages, the Vikings used merchant ships called "knorrs." They were tubbier and deeper than warships such as the Gok-

Trondheim in Norway. Near here, the Vikings were in the correct latitude to start their Atlantic crossings.

stad ship, which meant they could carry animals and cargo.

It was possible to row a knorr, but most of the time the ship relied on its sail. However, it could not sail into the wind but had to have the wind behind it. The direction of the wind, therefore, was very important and could affect the outcome of a journey.

The Vikings had no compasses and may not have had any navigation instruments. How, then, did they find their way? These instructions on how to reach Greenland give some idea:

From Hernar in Norway sail due west. Sail to the north of Shetland so that you can just see it in clear weather. Keep to the south of the Faroes so that the sea seems to be halfway up the mountains. Steer south of Iceland so that you can see birds and whales from there.

The Vikings could not start an Atlantic crossing from just anywhere. In order to reach the correct latitude, they had to sail first to Hernar, which is between modern Bergen and Trondheim. Then the ship stayed in the same latitude for the whole voyage on a course that the Vikings could keep with the help of the sun. They looked at it at noon each day and, as long as it appeared at the same height above the horizon, they were keeping to the right latitude. At night they would guide themselves by the stars.

In a fog or a storm, the Vikings were lost and might go around in circles for days. Iceland was found by a ship that had gone astray. Now came an even more important discovery, which may have been made in much the same way.

CHAPTER 12

Landfall in America

L'Anse aux Meadows in northern Newfoundland where traces of a Viking settlement were discovered by archaeologists in 1960. This site proves conclusively that the Vikings landed in North America

As related in the last chapter the Vikings crossed the Atlantic in stages, rather like going over a stream on stepping stones. First, they sailed to the islands north of Scotland — the Orkneys, the Shetlands, and the Faroes — next, they went to Iceland and after that to Greenland. Eventually, they reached America.

The sagas contain several stories about the Vikings in America, but it must be remembered that the sagas are sometimes fact, sometimes fiction, and often a mixture of both. One of these stories is about a merchant named Bjarni Herjulfsson, who traded between Iceland and Norway. He liked to spend the winter with his father in Iceland. When he arrived there in 985, he learned that the old man had moved to Greenland. Bjarni sailed off to find him.

On the voyage, Bjarni ran into gales and a fog and was soon lost. After several days, the weather improved, and Bjarni saw land but knew it was not Greenland. He had been told that Greenland had high mountains covered with snow, and there were none here. Moreover, he was fairly sure he had been driven too far west. His crew begged him to land there, but he refused. He guessed that Greenland must lie to the northeast, so he set sail in that direction. Three times more he sighted land, but he still refused to go ashore. At last, he reached Greenland, where he found his father. Bjarni's unwillingness to land cost him fame, since, had he done so, he would have been the first European to reach America.

MARKLAND AND VINLAND

Bjarni told his story to one of Eric the Red's sons, known as Leif the Lucky. Leif was curious to see the new lands for himself, so he bought Bjarni's vessel and set sail. The *Greenland Saga* says:

The first land they saw was the country Bjarni had seen last. They sailed close to the shore, dropped anchor, lowered a boat, and landed. There was no grass anywhere. Close by there were glaciers. The land between the glaciers and the sea was just a slab of rock. It all looked quite worthless.

Leif called this place "Helluland," or "Slab Land." Probably, it was part of Baffin Island. Leif and his friends did not think much of Slab Land, but their arrival there was a great moment in history.

Leif sailed on, soon reaching more land. As it was covered with trees, he called it "Markland," or "Forest Land." It may have been part of Labrador.

The Vikings went still farther south, pleased to find that, as they did so, the weather became warmer. Finally, they reached a place where they felt they could spend the winter. The saga says:

The rivers and lakes were full of salmon, the largest salmon they had ever seen. There was no frost in the winter, so the grass did not wither. They did not need fodder for their animals. Night and day were more equal in length than in Iceland or Greenland.

There was a German with the Vikings named Tyrkir who, one day, rushed into the camp babbling with excitement. He had found grapes growing wild! Leif decided to call this new country "Vinland" or "Wineland." There is no knowing where Vinland was, although some think it was part of New England. In any event, it must have been a long way south.

The following spring, Leif and his crew sailed home. Before leaving, they loaded their ship with timber, a valuable cargo for them, since there are no trees in Greenland.

CLASHES WITH NATIVE AMERICANS

Two more of Eric the Red's sons went exploring in America, the first of whom, Thorvald, reached land. He and his men found what they thought were three lumps on the shore, although they turned out to be canoes. Under each canoe three Native Americans were hiding. Thorvald's companions killed all of them, save one, who escaped to tell the rest of his tribe what had happened. Soon, many Native Americans were attacking the Vikings with bows and arrows. Although they killed only one of their enemies, that man was Thorvald.

The second of Eric the Red's sons, Thorstein, got lost at sea. Eventually he returned to Greenland, where he soon died.

In 1009 an Icelander named Thorfinn Karlsefni arrived in Greenland where he met Leif the Lucky and Thorstein's widow, Gudrid. They told him about Vinland, and he decided to settle there with Gudrid, for she and Thorfinn had married. Gudrid was to have a baby in America, the first European to be born there. Another woman in the party was Eric the Red's daughter, Freydis, a woman who, like her father, had great courage but also a dreadful temper.

Thorfinn found a land where there were grapes and wild wheat, so he decided this must be Vinland, and the Vikings camped there for the winter. However, it was much colder than

they expected; food was short, and they suffered badly from hunger.

Thorfinn and most of the Vikings were Christians, but among them was a pagan named Thorhall. One day he went off on his own to chant some spells. Shortly afterward, a whale came ashore. The Vikings now had all the meat they needed. Thorhall told them about his spells, boasting that the whale was a gift from Thor, who was much better than the Christian god. The Christian Vikings threw away their meat in disgust.

In the spring, the Vikings sailed farther south until they reached a land which, in addition to grapes and wild wheat, had plenty of fish and game, and good grass for the animals. They decided to stay there, calling the place Hop.

The following year, an enormous number of Native Americans appeared. But they only want-

Tyrkir discovers grapes in the country which the Vikings called Vinland.

ed to trade and offered the Vikings beautiful furs. In return, the Vikings gave them odds and ends of red cloth. All might have been well, but one of the Vikings' bulls broke loose and charged among the Native Americans, putting them to flight.

Thorfinn now built a stockade to protect his settlement. But the Native Americans attacked and caught the Vikings outside the fence. The Viking men were ready to flee, but Freydis, Eric the Red's daughter, called them cowards. Picking up a dead man's sword, she rushed at the Native Americans. It was the Native Americans who ran. The Vikings now returned to the place where they had spent the first winter. Here, the men quarreled over the women, and soon they all sailed back to Greenland.

Some years later, Freydis made another trip to Vinland with her husband and two groups of men and women. Although it was agreed they should share anything they found, a quarrel broke out which ended in violence. Freydis and her followers crept into the camp of the second group, pulled the men from their tents, and killed them one by one. When her men refused to kill the five women in the group, Freydis seized an ax and chopped them to pieces herself. She then took her people back to Greenland. She tried to prevent them from talking, but Leif the Lucky found out what she had done. Even so, he did not punish her.

TRACES OF THE VIKINGS

There is no record of any more voyages to Vinland. The people of Greenland were few, struggling to survive, so they were unable to found a new colony. But they may have visited Markland from time to time to collect much-needed timber.

Besides the saga tales, we have other evidence of the Vikings in America. In 1960 a Norwegian explorer named Helge Ingstad found a group of strange mounds at L'Anse aux Meadows, on the northern tip of Newfoundland. Helge's wife Anne was an archaeologist, so they both excavated the site. Soon, they were sure they had found a Viking settlement. There were eight houses, just the same shape as Viking longhouses, and there was even a sauna bath. They also found several small objects, among them a spindle whorl, a bronze pin with a ring head, and a stone lamp. All these objects were of the Viking type. Moreover, some distance from the houses was a smithy, with a furnace for smelting iron, an anvil, and a forge. As neither the Native Americans nor the Inuit knew anything about working in metal, the forge could not possibly have belonged to them.

The finds at L'Anse aux Meadows prove beyond a doubt that the Vikings went to America. What is less certain is that they had all the adventures described in the sagas.

*Vikings trading cloth with
Native Americans in exchange for furs.*

CHAPTER 13

The Vikings in Russia

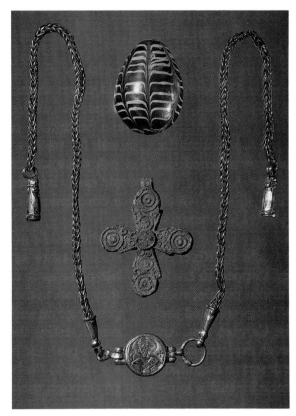

*Jewelry from Kiev
that was excavated in Sweden.*

Russia is a vast country, much of which, in the ninth century, belonged to tribes who were not very strong and who were fighting one another. For this reason, it was a tempting land for the Vikings to invade. Moreover, Russia has many great rivers which allowed them to travel wherever they wanted. They began by sailing up the rivers that flow into the Baltic Sea. Then they simply took their boats out of the water. They were able to drag or carry their boats overland to the rivers that flow to the Black Sea and the Caspian Sea. To the people they met, the Vikings were known as "the Rus," which may mean "the rowers," and this perhaps is how Russia got its name.

According to legend, the Russian people asked the Vikings to come and rule them. A chronicle says of the Russian tribes:

They quarreled and fought among themselves. And they said to themselves, "Let us find a king to rule over us." And they crossed the sea to the Rus. And they said to the Rus, "Our land is large and rich, but there is no order in it. Come and be king and rule over us."

Three Viking brothers then visited Russia. One ruled in Beloozero, another in Izborsk, and the third, named Rurik, in Novgorod. There must be some truth in this story, for archaeologists have found Viking goods in many Russian towns. The first Vikings seem to have arrived in about 840.

TRADE AND TRIBUTE

After Rurik died, a Viking named Oleg governed Novgorod and, around 880, seized Kiev, making this city his capital. There is a strange story about Oleg's death. According to a prophecy, his favorite horse would kill him. When the animal died first, Oleg was so relieved that he stamped on its skull, breaking it. A snake then crawled out of the skull and gave him a fatal bite.

After taking Novgorod and Kiev, some of the Vikings raided the area around the Caspian Sea. To reach it, they had to go by way of Khazaria. As this country was too strong for them to attack, they made a bargain with its ruler, promising that if he would let them through, he could have half of what they took on the Caspian.

The Vikings roamed everywhere around the Caspian, killing the peaceful inhabitants, burning and looting at will. Loaded with plunder, they left for home. But the Caspian folk were Muslims, and when their fellow Muslims, the

Khazars, heard what had happened, they became so furious that their ruler could not control them. They caught the Viking raiders as they traveled through and, in a three-day battle, killed nearly all of them.

The Viking towns in Russia, somewhat like those they built in England and Ireland, contained a fort surrounded by houses where many people lived and worked. In the countryside outside the towns were Russian tribes from whom the Vikings exacted tribute. In the north, this tribute consisted of furs, while in the south, it was wax and honey. And everywhere, the Vikings captured slaves.

The Vikings traded these goods for silver. In about 900, a silver mine was opened in Afghanistan and, as a result, the Arabs of the Middle East had large quantities of silver, which the Vikings wanted. The Arabs traded their silver quite happily for slaves.

The Vikings sailed down the Volga River to meet the Arabs. Often, they stopped to trade part of the way along with various people, such as the Bulghars, but other Vikings traveled the full length of the river to the Caspian Sea. An Arab writer says that a few even explored south of the Caspian, crossing the desert to Baghdad. They would have needed camels for such a journey, and although it is hard to imagine Vikings riding camels, it may have happened.

After about 950, the silver mines of Afghanistan were exhausted. The Vikings no longer did as much trade with the Arabs. Instead of sailing down the Volga to the Caspian, they now ventured down the Dnieper to the Black Sea.

A HOSTILE LAND

Merchants often gathered at Kiev so that they could travel together, for the voyage down the Dnieper was dangerous. In the first place, there was a fierce tribe called the Pechenegs, who lay in wait for traders, hoping to rob them. Another risk was a stretch of seven rapids where boats could easily be wrecked and men drowned. This is a description of the first of the rapids:

In the middle of the river are high rocks. The water dashes against them, making a terrible noise as it crashes down. The Rus take their boats to the bank and make many of their people go on shore. Some walk into the water naked, testing the bottom with their feet while others push the boat forward with poles, keeping close to the bank. So, with great care, they go through these first rapids.

At one point, the Vikings unloaded their boats, put their slaves into chains, and got them to carry their goods overland for six miles. The Vikings

Passing the rapids on the Dnieper River.

then returned to the boats, which they had to drag and carry over the same route. All the time they had to be on their guard, for this was where the Pechenegs were most likely to attack.

Soon after the rapids, the Vikings reached St. Gregor's Island. Now that the most dangerous part of their journey was over, they sacrificed cockerels to give thanks to their gods. From the mouth of the Dnieper they then sailed across the Black Sea to Constantinople, the journey from Kiev having taken between five and six weeks.

Today Constantinople is known as Istanbul and is the biggest city in Turkey. In the Viking age, it was the capital of a great empire called Byzantium, and most of its inhabitants were Greeks.

GALLEYS AND GREEK FIRE

The Vikings first reached Constantinople in about 840. They must have been amazed, since they came from dirty little wooden towns, and here was a splendid city built in stone and marble, defended by powerful walls. Above all, it was very wealthy. As soon as they saw it, the Vikings longed to plunder it.

The first Viking attack, in 860, was led by two men from Kiev, Askold and Dir. They chose their time well, for the emperor of Byzantium was hundreds of miles away fighting a war, and had left hardly any soldiers in Constantinople. Askold and Dir made the usual Viking assault, very sudden and very fierce. The people in the city were terrified. Calling on the Virgin Mary to protect them, they paraded what they believed to be her robes around the walls. The bishop of Constantinople dipped these clothes in the sea, whereupon there was a great storm which scattered the Viking fleet. All we know for certain is that Askold and Dir failed to take the city.

The Vikings attacked Constantinople again in 941, and once more the emperor was away with most of his army. He had left behind some old galleys. They were in very poor condition, but because they were all the defenders had, they fitted them out for war. Luckily, they also had a dangerous weapon, called Greek fire. It was made from sulfur, saltpeter, and petroleum. It blazed fiercely and was very difficult to put out. Even

Exotic eastern vessels that belonged to Vikings living in Russia.

if it fell in the sea, it floated and went on burning. The Greeks squirted their fire through iron tubes with ends shaped like dragons' heads, which has given us the myth that dragons breathe fire.

Confident that they could defeat a few old galleys, the Vikings sailed toward their enemies. But this is what happened:

As they lay surrounded by their foes, the Greeks began to fling their fire. Seeing the flames, the Rus jumped from their ships. They thought it better to drown than to burn alive. Some sank to the bottom under the weight of their armor. Some caught fire as they swam among the waves.

Having failed to take Constantinople, the Vikings ran wild in the countryside, burning villages and monasteries, and killing anyone they could find.

The Vikings suffered badly in all their wars with the Greeks. Usually, therefore, they were wise enough to trade rather than fight. They still sold the same goods, mainly furs and slaves. In return, the Greeks gave them all sorts of luxuries, such as jewelry and wine. What the Vikings prized most of all was Byzantine silk.

49

CHAPTER 14

Byzantium

The city of Constantinople had been named after the Roman Emperor Constantine, who founded it in the year 330. Later, in 395, the Roman Empire was divided, Rome being the capital of the western half while Constantinople was the capital of the eastern half, which became known as Byzantium. The western empire was overrun by invaders in the fifth century, but Byzantium lasted until 1453, when the Turks took Constantinople. They eventually gave it its present name, Istanbul.

Constantinople was built on a peninsula, so it had water on three sides. To the south was the Sea of Marmara and to the east the Bosporus. To the north, a deep bay called the Golden Horn made a splendid harbor, with an entrance that could be easily closed with a chain.

WEALTH FROM TRADE

Constantinople was well placed for trade, its merchants traveling all over the Mediterranean and the Black Sea. They also went through the Middle East where they met other merchants who sold goods from India and China. In the last chapter it was shown how the Vikings brought slaves and furs from Russia.

Trade made Constantinople rich, and many people chose to live there. Few towns in those days had more than a thousand inhabitants, yet Constantinople had half a million. Most of them were Greeks, and the official language was

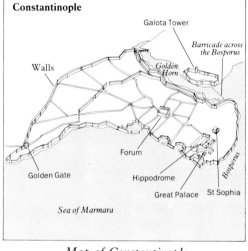

Map of Constantinople.

Greek, but there were people in the city from all over Europe, the Middle East, and North Africa.

Constantinople was well defended. On its west side were powerful walls, more than 26 feet (8 meters) tall, and with towers every 200 feet (60 meters). In front of them was a deep ditch. Thanks to their strong defensive walls and their secret weapon, Greek fire, the Byzantines had prevented the Vikings from capturing Constantinople several times.

Near the tip of the peninsula was a large square, having, in its center, a golden milestone from which all distances in the empire were measured. Around the square stood the emperor's Great Palace, the Senate House, some public baths, and the Hippodrome. In the Hippodrome, the Byzantines held chariot races and played polo, but they also had circus games, which included fights between gladiators and between humans and wild animals. Traitors and deserters were brought here to be shown to the people, who jeered and booed. One way of punishing a man was to dress him as a woman, sit him backward on a donkey, and then lead him round the arena. Heretics were burned alive in the Hippodrome, and the heads of executed criminals were sometimes displayed.

The Hippodrome contained enough seats for a huge crowd. When the emperor arrived to take his place in the royal box, the people either cheered or hooted, for it was the only chance they had of showing what they thought of him.

A wide, tree-lined avenue, with shops and

bazaars, ran west from the main square. This avenue led through several forums, or marketplaces, until, after three miles, it reached the main entrance to the city called the Golden Gate.

Water was brought to Constantinople by aqueducts. As an enemy could destroy these during a siege, local engineers had built enormous cisterns. Each was the size of a modern public swimming pool. Some cisterns were open to the sky while others were underground, their roofs being held up by columns. After they had taken the city, the Turks named one of these the "Cistern of a Thousand Columns."

The Cathedral of St. Sophia, one of the two great buildings of Constantinople.

CATHEDRAL AND PALACE

The two finest buildings in Constantinople were the cathedral of St. Sophia and the Great Palace.

The cathedral had been built on the orders of the Emperor Justinian and was finished in 537, after 10,000 men had worked on it for six years. It is still there, although it is now used as a museum. The dome, which is 170 feet (52 meters) high, stood for Heaven; the area below it stood for Paradise, that is, the Holy Land in the time of Jesus; and the lowest part stood for

A stone frieze representing the Byzantine emperor at the Hippodrome. Below him are spectators and dancers.

the world in which they lived at the time.

Twenty tons of silver ornamented St. Sophia, and other decorations were marble panels and mosaics. The mosaics, which showed scenes from the Bible, were made of marble, colored glass, and gold. The church was lit by great banks of candles. Around the gallery is a marble handrail, and on it some Viking runes have been discovered. Most of them have been badly worn, but it is possible to make out the letters A-L-F-D-A-N. Halfdan was a common Viking name. Carving your name where you should not is a very old habit.

The Great Palace was a large area surrounded by a wall. Inside the wall was not one palace but seven, and there were also halls, conference rooms, churches, and chapels. The palace precinct contained stables for racehorses, riding horses, chargers, and polo ponies, kennels for the dogs and cheetahs that the emperor used for hunting, cages for falcons, and even a private zoo. In all, 20,000 guards and servants worked in the Great Palace, so it resembled a large town.

THE EMPEROR ON SHOW

Everything was done to make the emperor of Byzantium look important. The heir to the throne was born in a room hung with purple silk, the most expensive cloth there was. Today the expression "born in the purple" means that someone has very rich and powerful parents.

When an emperor was crowned, he wore robes which, it was said, angels had given to Constantine the Great. The emperor was sometimes called the "thirteenth apostle." Priests told the people that their emperor had been divinely chosen so that to disobey him was a sin against God.

From time to time there were magnificent processions at which the emperor wore his crown and his coronation robes, his guards wore shining armor, and his courtiers were dressed in silk.

There were elaborate ceremonies. A royal birth, marriage, or death was a great occasion, as were church festivals and public holidays. There were so many royal and public occasions, and they were so complicated, that nobody could remember them all, and they had to be written down in a Book of Ceremonies.

The emperor had a special throne, intended to impress visitors from abroad. Bishop Liutprand, an ambassador from Cremona in Italy, described it in the year 948:

> Before the emperor's throne stood a tree. It was made of bronze gilded over. Its branches were filled with birds, also made of gilded bronze. Each kind gave a different cry.
>
> The throne itself was huge and wonderfully made. At one moment it was low on the ground; at another moment it rose high in the air. It was guarded by lions, made of bronze covered with gold, who beat the ground with their tails and opened their mouths to roar.
>
> Two servants brought me to the emperor, and at once the lions began to roar and the birds to sing. I knelt before the emperor, bowing my face to the ground three times. Then I raised my head. The man who had been just in front of me was now as high as the ceiling. How it was done I could not imagine.

Today we would not be amazed by metal birds that sang, metal lions that roared, and a seat that shot up in the air, for we see that kind of thing at fairgrounds. But a thousand years ago, few

The emperor's mechanical throne, which so impressed Bishop Liutprand.

The return of the Varangians. Their marvelous clothes were a sensation in the Viking homelands.

people knew of anything more complicated than a potter's wheel, so the throne of the emperor of Byzantium must have looked like magic.

THE VARANGIAN GUARD

In spite of everything, the emperor lived in fear of being overthrown. Should that happen, he knew he would lose something. If he was lucky, it might only be his freedom, and he would be forced to live in a monastery. If he was unlucky, he might lose his ears and his nose, although most likely it would be his eyes. Constantine VI, for example, drove his mother into exile, but she returned, seized power, and blinded her own son.

The emperor of Byzantium needed soldiers to protect him. For this duty, he had several regiments of guards, one of which was called the "Varangians," a word meaning "barbarians." Most of the Varangians were Vikings. The emperor chose them because they were good soldiers and, being foreigners, they were not interested in the quarreling and plotting that went on in Constantinople. They had simply taken

an oath of loyalty to the emperor and, being men of their word, they could be relied upon to defend him with their lives, as long as the emperor was loyal to them in return.

The following is a description of some Varangians, Bolli Bollason and his friends, who were returning to Iceland after they had been in Byzantium for several years:

They were all wearing clothes of scarlet cloth. They sat on gilded saddles. All were fine men, but Bolli outdid the rest. He wore clothes of silk and had on a scarlet cloak. He was wearing his sword Legbiter. Its hilt was decorated with gold, and it had gold thread round the grip. On his head was a gilded helmet. He had a scarlet shield on his side, with a knight painted on it in gold. He carried a lance, as they do in foreign lands.

Wherever they went, the women could do nothing but stare at Bolli and his friends.

Obviously, any young Viking who saw these striking men would be eager to join the Varangian Guard.

CHAPTER 15

Harald Hardrada

In 1031 a boy of sixteen arrived at the court of King Yaroslav of Kiev. He was Harald Hardrada, the half brother of St. Olaf, who had fled after his defeat in the Battle of Sticklestad the previous year. Yaroslav was always ready to welcome a promising young soldier, so Harald joined his army and helped him in a war against the Poles. King Yaroslav had a beautiful daughter, Elizabeth, whom Harald wanted to marry, but she said he must first prove he was worthy of her. So he decided to seek his fortune in the great city of Constantinople.

Harald arrived in the city in 1035. At that time the emperor was Michael IV, and his wife was the Empress Zoe. They allowed Harald to join the Varangian Guard. He soon won the respect of his fellow guards and also gained the favor of the emperor, who made him an officer.

TREASURE AND TORTURE

Among the many Viking sagas written down by Snorri Sturluson is *King Harald's Saga*, which is the story of Harald Hardrada. It tells many exciting tales about him when he served with the Varangians. Here are some of them.

Harald fought in several wars, one of which was against the Arabs, either in the Middle East or in North Africa. Harald is said to have taken 80 cities.

Later, Harald fought in Sicily, where he also captured a number of cities. Snorri describes some of the sieges.

Once, Harald's men dug beneath the walls of a town, working away until they were under some flagstones. A group of the men then burst through. They came up in the middle of a large hall, where many of the townsfolk were eating breakfast. The people fled in terror while the Varangians rushed to the gates and opened them to let in the rest of their army.

Another town was also protected by strong walls, but its houses had thatched roofs. The sparrows that nested in the thatch flew out of the town every day to feed in the woods, and Harald ordered his men to capture some of them. They smeared wood shavings with wax and brimstone, tied them to the birds, and set fire to them. The birds flew to their nests, setting fire to the thatch so that the whole town was burned to the ground.

Snorri also says that Harald conquered Palestine, where he killed many robbers. This made it safe for pilgrims to travel to Jerusalem.

Wherever he fought, Harald took plunder. He was supposed to give much of it to the emperor, but he kept more than a fair share for himself. He sent this treasure to honest King Yaroslav, who looked after it for him.

In 1041 Harald was put in prison, probably for keeping too much plunder. Shortly after his arrest, Michael IV died, and his nephew, another Michael, became emperor. Instead of ruling alongside Zoe, he had her head shaved and shut her away in a nunnery. Moreover, Michael was such a cruel man and governed so badly that the people of Constantinople rebelled.

Michael V had made a serious error, for he had not won over the Varangians. As they still had loyal feelings for the Empress Zoe, they joined the revolt. During the revolt, Harald escaped from prison, to be welcomed by the Varangians as their leader.

Michael V and his uncle took refuge in a

Harald escapes from Constantinople. The boat is mounting the chain, so the men must now rush forward to make it tip over the other side.

church, but the Varangians dragged them into the street and blinded them both. Although the uncle lay quietly while he was tortured, Michael screamed and struggled so much that he had to be bound. It may well have been Harald who gouged out his eyes.

Harald now decided it was time to return to Norway. Because he had yet another load of treasure to smuggle out, he attempted to escape in secret, after dark. That posed a problem, however, as the harbor of Constantinople was closed by a chain at night. Harold ordered his men to row as hard as they could toward the chain. As they drew near, some of the crew moved to the back of the boat. The bows shot up above the chain. The men now ran forward, and the boat slid over the top of the obstacle. A second boat tried to perform the same trick, but it broke its keel, and most of the crew drowned. Harald then made his way back to Kiev. Here he married Elizabeth, collected his treasure, and left for Norway.

We do not know how many of these stories from *King Harald's Saga* are to be believed, especially since several of them are told of other men as well. There is, however, a Greek chronicle that also mentions Harald. It says that he came to Constantinople, joined the army, and was promoted to high rank. It states, too, that he fought in Sicily, and that he left Constantinople secretly. The chronicle thus confirms all the important facts given in the saga. But did Harald really capture 80 Arab cities? Did he use burning sparrows to destroy a town? Did he personally gouge out an emperor's eyes? There may be some truth in these tales, but we cannot be sure.

KING OF NORWAY

When Harald returned to Scandinavia, his nephew, Magnus the Good, was king of both Norway and Denmark. Harald, greedy for power, felt that Magnus should hand over one of these countries, so he gathered an army in Sweden and prepared to invade Norway. Magnus, however, wanted peace. He offered Harald a share in the throne of Norway if, in return, Harald gave him half the treasure he had brought from Constantinople. Harald agreed.

When the two men met in 1046, Magnus declared that Harald should also be king of Norway. Harald's followers then brought in several chests, emptying their contents onto a large ox hide spread on the ground. The immense quantity of gold and silver amazed everyone. It was all carefully weighed, and Magnus and Harald took half each. They ruled Norway jointly for several years. Then Magnus died, so that Harald alone was king.

THE BATTLE OF THE NISSA

Harald also had designs on Magnus's other kingdom, Denmark, but before he could invade it, a man named Sweyn Ulfsson seized power. Harald at once declared war on Sweyn. The Norwegians attacked Denmark again and again, doing a great deal of damage. On one of their raids they

Harald shares his treasure with King Magnus.

burned the important town of Hedeby.

Once, Sweyn's fleet surprised Harald's. The Danes had more ships than the Norwegians who, because they were carrying heavy loads of plunder and prisoners, could not row fast. To reduce weight and gain speed, Harald ordered his men to throw the Danish prisoners overboard. While Sweyn's men stopped to rescue their friends, Harald's fleet escaped.

In 1062 there was a great sea fight known as the Battle of the Nissa. Both sides roped many of their ships together, making platforms on which the men fought, just as they would have done on land. Other ships were left untied so that they could maneuver freely and give help wherever it was needed.

According to *King Harald's Saga*, the Danes had 300 ships and the Norwegians 150, but in spite of their inferior numbers, the Norwegians won. Harald Hardrada fought bravely, as always, but the real hero on the Norwegian side was Earl Hakon. He commanded some of the vessels that had not been roped, using them to capture one Danish ship after another. Also, he rescued part of the Norwegian fleet which was under heavy pressure from the enemy.

Harald was far from pleased at having to yield battle honors to Hakon. He was angered even more at receiving the news that Hakon had helped Sweyn Ulfsson to escape. Harald immediately launched an attack on Hakon's lands and defeated him in battle. Hakon fled, leaving his followers at Harald's mercy. Harald killed some, maimed others, and drove most of the remainder from their farms.

In 1064 Harald and Sweyn signed a pact whereby Harald agreed that Sweyn should keep Denmark. The war had lasted for seventeen years, but Harald had gained nothing.

THE HARD RULER

Harald ruled Norway with an iron hand. People in his presence had to stand or sit, just as he decreed, visitors had to bow low before him, and he punished severely anyone who disobeyed him. In addition to being strict, Harald was treacherous. After he quarreled with a nobleman called Einar Paunch-Shaker, the two men agreed to hold talks to settle their dispute. Harald darkened the room where they were to meet, and his men killed Einar as soon as he entered.

Einar's followers were so furious that they were ready to rebel against Harald, but a man named Finn Arnason persuaded them to keep the peace. Harald rewarded Finn by allowing his brother, Kalf Arnason, to return to Norway. Harald believed that Kalf had killed King Olaf at the Battle of Sticklestad, but now he promised to forgive him. Later, Kalf accompanied Harald on a raid against Denmark. Harald ordered Kalf to take his men ashore first and lead the attack, saying he would follow with the main army. But Harald deliberately did not land with his men until Kalf had been killed. After that, Finn Arnason fought for the Danes.

The Battle of the Nissa, A.D. 1062, in which the Norwegians defeated the Danes.

Harald, nevertheless, had some redeeming features. He built two churches at Trondheim; when there was a famine in Iceland he sent food; and after capturing Finn Arnason at the Battle of the Nissa, he set him free, although Finn insulted him. He often rewarded followers who were loyal to him; and when not engaged in warfare, he would sometimes compose poems.

CHAPTER 16

Harald Invades England

In 1043 the English chose Edward the Confessor as their king. Because he was only interested in religious matters, he left the government of the country to Harold, Earl of Wessex. Two other important noblemen were Tostig, Earl of Northumbria, who was Harold's brother, and Morcar, Earl of Mercia.

Edward the Confessor had spent many years in Normandy, and he gave some of his Norman friends influential positions at court. Moreover, when, in 1052 Duke William of Normandy visited England, Edward promised him that he would be the next king of England. The English were angry and alarmed.

We know something about the history of these years from the Bayeux Tapestry, which shows what happened in pictures, with a few words to explain them. We see Earl Harold going to Normandy, being taken to Duke William, and later, fighting in William's army, against the Bretons. Before sailing back to England, Harold made some kind of oath.

The tapestry does not say why Harold went to Normandy, although he might have been shipwrecked. Nor do we know exactly what oath Harold took, but probably, he was made to swear that he would help William become king of England.

A DOUBLE THREAT

In 1065 the people of Northumbria rebelled against

The coronation of Harold of England as recorded in the Bayeux Tapestry.

Tostig and asked Edwin, brother of Morcar, to be their earl. Tostig fled abroad, especially angry because Harold, his own brother, did nothing to help him.

Edward the Confessor died in January 1066 and, since the English nobles wanted a strong ruler, they chose Harold as their king. William of Normandy at once gathered an army and built ships. Harold, too, assembled an army and a fleet, although many of his men deserted through lack of food, and his ships were lost in a storm.

Meanwhile, Tostig had taken refuge with Harald Hardrada in Norway. Harald had always hoped to be king of England, but had done nothing about it because he had been busy fighting the Danes. Now the war with Denmark was over, and Tostig had arrived, promising to help him. Harald gathered a fleet of ships, filled them with men, and set sail for England.

Before he left, Harald visited the shrine of St. Olaf, hoping the saint would assist him in the war with England. Olaf's beard and nails were still growing, so Harald cut them. He did this out of respect, to make the corpse look neat and well-groomed, and to win the saint's support for his invasion.

The Vikings had several bad omens. One of the men in Harald's fleet dreamed he saw an ugly witch holding a knife and boasting that she would feast on the flesh of dead warriors. Another dreamed of a wolf, with blood dripping from its jaws and swallowing men as fast as it could. And Harald himself had a dream in which St. Olaf came to him and said:

Now I am afraid, great Harald,
That death is waiting for you
And wolves will tear your body.

Harald first sailed to Orkney and Shetland, where he gained more local support, so that he now had 300 ships and 9,000 men. With this force he landed in Yorkshire, where the army surrounded Scarborough. The men lit a bonfire and flung blazing wood from it on the thatched roofs of the houses. As the people fled, the Vikings killed them. King Harold of England was in the south, expecting the Normans. When he heard of the Yorkshire invasion, he hurried north with his troops.

THE BATTLE OF STAMFORD BRIDGE

Earls Edwin and Morcar tried to stop Harald Hardrada from taking York and blocked his way at Gate Fulford. Harald hoisted his banner, which he called "Land Waster," and led his army into the attack. Both sides fought fiercely until the English fled.

Harald now captured York, and its people, who were descendants of the original Vikings, promised to help him conquer the rest of England. Harald also took hostages from the English nobles who lived in the north.

On September 25, 1066, Harald Hardrada's fleet was on the Ouse River, near Riccall. About a third of his army was guarding it, while the rest of his men were thirteen miles away at Stamford Bridge. They were resting and,

Harold of England is killed at the Battle of Hastings. A scene from the Bayeux Tapestry.

as it was a warm day, many removed their armor. Suddenly, a cloud of dust appeared in the distance. Tostig thought it might be Saxons coming to make their peace with Harald, but soon the Vikings saw the gleam of armor. It was Harold of England with his army. He had taken the resting Vikings completely by surprise.

Harald Hardrada quickly lined up his men. As he was riding to inspect them, his horse threw him. It looked like a bad omen, but Harald jumped up, saying, "A fall means good for-

Harald pares the nails and cuts the hair of St. Olaf.

The Battle of Stamford Bridge.

tune is on the way." The English king asked some Norwegians who were with him, "Who was that man who fell from his horse?" They told him it was Harald Hardrada, and he exclaimed, "What a big man he is! Let us hope his luck has run out now."

Harold, with a small party, rode toward the Viking army. He called to his brother Tostig, saying he could have back all his lands if he would change sides. "How much land will you give Harald of Norway," asked Tostig.

"He can have six feet of England," replied Harold. Then he added, "No, he can have seven feet, because he is so tall." Tostig remained with the Vikings.

When Harold of England had ridden back to his army, Harald Hardrada asked Tostig who he was. Tostig informed him, and Harald remarked, "What a little man he is! But how proudly he stood in his stirrups!"

The battle now began. The Derwent River lay between the two armies. There was a bridge over it, but the Vikings had sent hardly any men to defend it. A giant of a Norwegian held it for a while, killing forty Saxons with his battle ax, but then a Saxon crept below the bridge and stabbed him through a gap in the timbers. The Saxons poured across to attack their enemies.

Harald Hardrada "went berserk." In a wild rage, he flung his shield over his shoulder and swung his sword with both hands. His blows were so powerful that he sliced through helmets and coats of mail. No one could stand up to him. The Vikings appeared to be winning, but then Harald Hardrada was killed by a chance arrow. His men went on fighting bravely, taking heart when their friends from the ships arrived, but eventually they were all defeated. Harold allowed the survivors to return to Norway. Three hundred ships had invaded; only twenty-four now left.

THE NORMAN CONQUEST

Stamford Bridge was the greatest victory that the Saxons ever won over the Vikings. Nevertheless, the Vikings had done much harm, for they had destroyed the armies of earls Edwin and Morcar and had killed or wounded many of Harold's best men. Meanwhile, the Normans were ready to invade, awaiting only a favorable wind. Harold's weakened army would have to resist them on its own.

The Normans landed at Pevensey on September 28, three days after Stamford Bridge. Harold led his army south by forced marches, and a fierce battle was fought at Senlac Hill near Hastings. The Normans won, Harold was killed, and Duke William of Normandy became king of England.

60

CHAPTER 17

The End of the Viking Age

Harald Hardrada's invasion of England was the last time the Vikings tried to conquer another country. Groups of Vikings continued raiding while, in their homelands, life went on as before. Nonetheless, the Viking Age came to an end at the Battle of Stamford Bridge in 1066. Why was this?

For hundreds of years the Vikings had attacked countries which could not defend themselves very successfully, but now that had changed. The Irish won the Battle of Clontarf, so ending the threat to their country. France, too, was safe, for the Normans, descended from the Vikings, protected the north coast. Now the Normans had conquered England.

The Vikings still tried some of their old tricks. In 1069 a Danish army landed, and the Vikings of northern England rebelled. Having persuaded the Danes to leave, William I took such dreadful revenge on the rebels that twenty years later much of Yorkshire was still like a desert.

It is said that the Viking Age ended because the Vikings became Christians. The Danes were converted in the tenth century after Bishop Poppo persuaded King Harald Bluetooth that Christ was more powerful than Odin. Poppo did so by putting his hand inside a red-hot iron glove and taking it out unharmed. Harald at once embraced Christianity and ordered his subjects to do the same.

In Norway, King Olaf Tryggvason likewise instructed the people to become Christians. After Olaf died in 1000, the Norwegians went back to their old gods. When Olaf the Stout was crowned king in 1014, he again ordered his subjects to accept Christianity.

In the end, most Vikings became Christians, more or less willingly. It did not make much difference to the way they behaved.

EPILOGUE

The Vikings were full of energy and courageous. They were excellent sailors and shipbuilders and wonderful artists and craftsmen. Not surprisingly, they have left us a great deal.

In the museums of Scandinavia are many beautiful objects, such as jewelry, weapons, and splendid ships. The Vikings have also given us a remarkable literature in their sagas, which are still exciting and entertaining to read.

Large numbers of Vikings settled in England, Ireland, France, and Russia. In parts of England and France there are still Viking place names. People in the north of England have their own accent and use dialect words that come from the Viking language, Old Norse. The Viking settlements in Russia, like Novgorod and Kiev, were to become the core of the modern state.

The Vikings kept their own identity in the lands that were uninhabited, namely, the Faroe Islands, Iceland, and Greenland. The settlements in the Faroes and Iceland have lasted until the present day. The one in Greenland died out early in the fifteenth century. We know the climate there became colder, so perhaps that killed them, or possibly, the Inuit took their revenge.

The greatest of the Vikings' achievements was to arrive in America, although they never realized the potential of their arrival. They failed to settle here and soon forgot about it. Europeans heard no more of America until Columbus sailed to the West Indies in 1492.

Perhaps the most important thing the Vikings have left us is their memory, that of a ferocious, cruel, but exceptionally brave and enterprising people.

Glossary

ANGLO-SAXONS People who lived in England during the Viking Age. These people came from Germany in the south and began to settle in England after the Romans left early in the fifth century. Often they are known simply as Saxons.

ASGARD City that was the home of the Viking gods.

BERSERK Particularly violent and savage Viking warrior.

CHRONICLE Diary of important events, usually kept by monks. The diary was written up every year.

DANEGELD Money paid by the Saxons as a bribe to the Vikings to leave them in peace.

ELL Measurement that varied at different times and in different countries. In England it was 45 inches.

FJORD Deep, steep-sided valley cut by a glacier and then invaded by the sea. The sides are so steep they are not inhabitable.

GREEK FIRE Inflammable mixture of sulfur, saltpeter, and petroleum used as a weapon by the Byzantines. They set it on fire and squirted it at their enemies.

HACK SILVER Fragments of silver ornaments and coins that were hacked up to make smaller amounts of change.

HOMAGE Promise made to serve and obey a monarch or a lord.

JOMSVIKINGS Men between the ages of eighteen and fifty who lived by raiding and plundering like the Vikings. Their homes were fortresses where women were not allowed.

KEEL The level timber that runs along the middle and bottom of a ship and looks like its backbone.

KNORR Viking merchant ship.

MEAD Alcoholic drink made with honey and water.

NORSEMEN Another name for Vikings, also called Northmen.

PAGANS People who worshiped many gods; broadly, those who were neither Christians, Jews, nor Moslems.

REEVE Saxon official.

RELICS Remains of saints kept in churches or shrines: usually consisting of bones or pieces of clothing.

RIB Curved timber frame of a ship that runs from the keel to the deck and supports the planking.

RUNE Letter in the Viking alphabet.

SAGA Epic poem telling stories of Viking gods and heroes.

SAUNA Steam bath. The Vikings made the steam by pouring water on hot stones.

SKRAELING Viking name, meaning "savages," which they gave to the Inuit and Native Americans.

STEM Timber at the very front of a ship, where the planks meet.

STERN POST Timber at the back of a ship.

VALHALLA The Viking heaven.

VARANGIANS Foreigners, mostly Vikings, who made up the guard of the emperor of Byzantium.

Index